Better Homes and Gardens.

501
Fun-to-Make
Family
Crafts

Better Homes and Gardens® Books
Des Moines, Iowa

Better Homes and Gardens® Books
An imprint of Meredith® Books

501 Fun-to-Make Family Crafts

Editor: Carol Field Dahlstrom
Technical Editor: Susan M. Banker
Graphic Designer: Angie Haupert Hoogensen
Copy and Production Editor: Terri Fredrickson
Book Production Managers: Pam Kvitne, Marjorie J. Schenkelberg
Contributing Copy Editor: Arianna McKinney
Contributing Proofreaders: Elizabeth Martin, Margaret Smith
Technical Illustrator: Chris Neubauer Graphics, Inc.
Electronic Production Coordinator: Paula Forest
Editorial and Design Assistants: Judy Bailey, Mary Lee Gavin, Karen Schirm

Meredith® Books
Editor in Chief: James D. Blume
Design Director: Matt Strelecki
Managing Editor: Gregory H. Kayko

Director, Retail Sales and Marketing: Terry Unsworth
Director, Sales, Special Markets: Rita McMullen
Director, Sales, Premiums: Michael A. Peterson
Director, Sales, Retail: Tom Wierzbicki
Director, Book Marketing: Brad Elmitt
Director, Operations: George A. Susral
Director, Production: Douglas M. Johnston

Vice President, General Manager: Jamie L. Martin

Better Homes and Gardens® Magazine
Editor in Chief: Jean LemMon
Executive Food Editor: Nancy Byal

Meredith Publishing Group
President, Publishing Group: Stephen M. Lacy
Vice President, Finance and Administration: Max Runciman

Meredith Corporation
Chairman and Chief Executive Officer: William T. Kerr

Chairman of the Executive Committee: E. T. Meredith III

All of us at Better Homes and Gardens® Books are dedicated to providing you
with information and ideas to create beautiful and useful projects.
We welcome your comments and suggestions.
Write to us at: Better Homes and Gardens Books, Crafts Editorial Department,
1716 Locust Street—LN112, Des Moines, IA 50309-3023.

If you would like to purchase any of our books, check wherever quality books are sold.
Visit our website at bhg.com.

get ready
to make
memories

Welcome to a crafting book that is so much more than a book about making things. This wonderful collection of make-it-together projects will inspire hours of family fun and laughter. You'll learn more about each other and share meaningful discussions. You'll learn new crafting techniques and boost your creativity. Ultimately, you'll experience the rewards of a loving family— holding dear the treasure of that gift. We know you'll like each of the projects in this book and that you'll love the memories you make as you craft together as a family.

Carol Field Dahlstrom

contents

autumn

When the glorious days of autumn roll around, it's the perfect time to incorporate nature into your crafting! When you go on your next hike, remember to take along a tote bag for gathering pinecones, fallen leaves, driftwood, and other outdoor finds—you just might need them for making a nature box, turkey character, or pumpkin wand!

winter

There are so many reasons to make things at the year's end. Make sure your crafts supplies are well-stocked! You'll find dozens of great ideas for holiday gifts and decorations in this festive chapter. Whether you'd like to make your own Christmas cards, clay menorah, New Year's party favors, or sweet valentines, you're sure to find favorite crafts the whole family will love making this winter.

spring
pages 142–193

As a fresh new season begins, enjoy every minute by setting aside some family crafting time. We'll share a basket full of ways to make springtime delights— such as wonderful Easter eggs, fantastic bugs and creatures, and oh-so-pretty barrettes using beads, ribbons, and chenille stems. You're sure to discover new techniques and favorite projects to celebrate spring!

summer
pages 194–219

Goodbye homework and grueling schedules; it's time to enjoy the carefree days of summer! Make the most of warm-weather days by learning a new crafting technique together. This chapter just might have you painting your favorite sandals or creating a scrapbook to capture all your splendid days in the sun.

how to use this book

Dear Parents,
We know that you and your family will love making the projects in this book. Take a minute to read about the special features of this book—then start crafting together.

about the projects...
The crafts in this book have been specially selected for families who want to spend time together making fun stuff. From painting, sewing, and printmaking to stamping, decoupaging, and beading, you'll find hundreds of great projects to make and enjoy. And to spark the imagination even more, we've provided page after page of alternative ideas to help personalize projects and take them one step further.

about the instructions...
Whether you have a crafting background or don't think you can draw a straight line, success is ensured with each of our projects. We walk you through each one with clear, concise, step-by-step instructions and helpful photographs when needed. Every project includes a complete materials list so you won't be caught without a supply once you've started. If a supply is a little out of the ordinary, we'll tell you where to find it, right in the materials list!

We encourage you to play right along with your child, as half the fun of crafting is in the sharing of the experience. Your assistance will often be needed when using a crafts knife or scissors, or in other steps that should be supervised or completed by an adult. Practicing and reinforcing safety are very important when teaching the fundamentals of crafting.

about the techniques...
This book includes a wide range of crafting techniques, including projects to paint, decoupage, print, bead, cross-stitch, and more. Each technique has been tested by professional crafts designers.

about the patterns...
You'll discover dozens of patterns to use when making the projects in this book. Whenever possible, the patterns are full-size to make them easy to use. Remember to refer to these patterns when designing your own creative projects. For instance, just refer to pages 136–137 the next time you want to make an "I love you" card or a keepsake valentine!

about the symbols...

For easy reference, the projects are grouped and labeled with symbols so you can find the type of project you want at a glance. Below and on pages 8 and 9, you'll find the symbols in the order they appear, color coded by season and an explanation of what the symbols mean. Watch for these symbols in the upper right-hand corner of each page spread:

nature projects
14–19

back-to-school projects
20–27

bird projects
28–31

sports projects
32–33

pumpkin decorations
34–43

halloween treat holders
44–49

halloween costumes
50–61

halloween party projects
62–67

thanksgiving projects
68–71

holiday cards
76–80

tree trims
81–97

stockings
98–101

symbols continued on page 8

about the symbols—continued

christmas decorations
102–103

holiday gifts
104–115

hanukkah projects
116–119

luminarias
120–121

snow projects
122–125

new year's projects
126–127

valentine projects
128–137

get-well projects
138–141

rain projects
146–147

bug projects
148–155

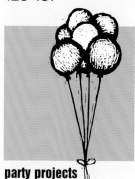

party projects
156–157

easter projects
158–163

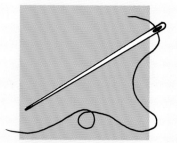

cross-stitch projects
164–165

jewelry making
166–169

tabletop projects
170–173

photo projects
174–175

mother's day gifts
176–185

birthday projects
186–187

father's day gifts
188–193

beach projects
198–199

flying insect projects
200–201

pet projects
202–209

seashell projects
210–211

musical instruments
212–213

travel projects
214–215

camping projects
216–217

photo display projects
218–219

autumn

As the crisp breezes of autumn begin to blow, it is the perfect time to rediscover nature. From a visit to the apple orchard to a hayrack ride through the pumpkin patch, come along as we celebrate this glorious time of year. With projects such as nature boxes and wire-laced pumpkins, the whole family will love crafting with favorite finds of the season.

crafting in autumn

When the seasons change, it is a reminder of the beauty that surrounds us each day. Autumn's glory inspires us to get in touch with nature—to linger over the unmistakable scent in the air, to stand in awe of the magnificent colors, and to use nature's gifts as inspiration for expressing our individual creativity. Come along and share ideas for making the most of autumn crafting.

◆ Take a nature walk to collect fallen treasures. Take along a tote bag or two to hold acorns, pinecones, sticks, leaves, feathers, driftwood, or other items to use when crafting.

◆ Teach the kids how to bargain shop and think ahead. For instance, shop for Halloween crafting supplies, decorations, and costumes the day after Halloween.

◆ Visit the library to find information on how to dry gourds. When dried, the unusual shapes are fun to paint and decorate for any season.

◆ Go on a family leaf hunt, gathering as many different kinds of leaves as you can find. Together learn from what trees the leaves have fallen. Then dry the leaves and spray-paint them in bright colors to use in decorating.

◆ Make an autumn wreath by using finds of the season. Hot-glue leaves, bittersweet, pinecones, small gourds, and other items to a grapevine wreath.

◆ Pumpkins not only make the perfect Halloween decoration but are also a welcome sight at Thanksgiving. To make sure you have some left for turkey day, buy a few extra at Halloween time and store them in a cool place until ready to display.

When school supplies are well-stocked in stores before school starts, keep your eye out for bright pencils, erasers, rulers, and other small items. Hot-glue them to a picture frame to make a fun back-to-school gift.

Before the snow falls, be sure to pick up all the fallen sticks in the yard. Use the sticks as accents on wreaths, in flower arrangements, and for snowman arms.

Designate a place where the kids can store crafting supplies and work on their projects. Remember to teach safety when using things such as scissors and hot-glue guns. Also keep newspapers and waxed paper on hand to protect work surfaces.

Have the kids make Thanksgiving cards for friends and family. Glue a leaf to card stock for the turkey's tail feathers and cut the head from construction paper. Add wiggly eyes, feet, and wattles for the finishing touches.

Visit a pumpkin patch or apple orchard to pick up pumpkins, gourds, and apples for holiday decorating and seasonal recipes.

Watch your local newspaper for places providing hayrack rides. These rides are great fun and give the whole family time away to laugh and talk. When you return home, have the kids draw a picture to remember the experience.

Start a school-year scrapbook. Purchase plain scrapbooks and let the kids decorate the covers.

Dried flowers work well in autumn arrangements. To enhance the colors, spray lightly with floral spray paint.

Have fun scouring flea markets and yard sales in search of wood crates and baskets. These items are perfect for displaying seasonal finds such as gourds, stalks of wheat, and Indian corn.

Start thinking of handmade treasures to make for Christmas and Hanukkah. Have supplies ready so you can get a jump start on holiday gift making.

For a lovely autumn centerpiece, make a pumpkin vase. Cut the top off the pumpkin and scoop out the insides. Add a plastic liner and then fill the pumpkin with dried flowers, berries, and sticks. If desired, tie a ribbon around the center of the pumpkin.

Apple-Print Linens

Set your table with welcome signs of the season—napkins and place mats embellished with striking apple motifs.

what you'll need

Apples
Sharp knife
Acrylic paints in apple green and red
Paper plate
Printer paper
Purchased fabric napkins and place mats
Permanent red marker

now make it together

1 On a cutting surface, cut an apple in half, cutting from the top to the bottom and leaving the stem on one side. Be sure to cut straight and smooth so the apple can be used for printing.

2 Place some paint on a paper plate. Dip the apple half with stem into the paint, saturating the apple and stem. Dab off on paper. Press where desired on a place mat or napkin. Carefully lift from the fabric.
Repeat, using desired color of paint. Let the paint dry.

3 Use a permanent marker to write phrases such as "An apple a day..." or "Good for you" on the napkin.

All-Aglow Apples

Visit a local orchard (or head to the grocery store) to pick the perfect apples for this clever autumn centerpiece that sparkles with the season's brilliance.

what you'll need

Variety of apples
Sharp knife
Hydrogen peroxide
Short taper candles
Metallic-color chenille stems
Scissors
Ruler
Colored beads
Sequins

Note: For safety, never leave a burning candle unattended.

now make it together

1 Choose a variety of apples with fairly symmetrical shapes. Wash and dry the apples.

2 Using a knife, cut a hole in center of apple to remove core. Pour hydrogen peroxide into the hole to prevent the apple from turning brown; drain. Insert a candle into the hole.

3 Cut several chenille stems to lengths ranging from 6 to 10 inches long. String different colored beads and sequins onto the chenille stems. Curl the ends of the stems if desired. Insert the embellished stems into the apples around candles.

Talk With Your Kids
....
Give your kids a safety quiz about lighting matches and using candles.

Autumn-Red Wreath

Striking with red celosia, this elegant wreath can be
created from any type of dried flowers.

what you'll need
Red celosia or other desired dried flowers
Rubber bands
Floral spray paints in desired colors
Scissors; 14-inch wire wreath form
Hot-glue gun and hot-glue sticks
Thick gold braid; gold ribbon

now make it together

1 If picking flowers for this project, gather
them when the blooms are fully developed. Remove leaves. Bundle several
flowers together with rubber bands and
hang upside down in a cool, dry place. After
drying, the flowers can be sprayed with red
floral spray paint to enhance the color if
desired. Trim the stems to measure between
4 and 8 inches.

2 Lay wreath form flat on work surface.
Begin gluing a layer of dried flowers on
the outer ring. Insert small stems into the
bottom ring and glue in place. Blooms
should extend 2 to 3 inches beyond the
form. Continue to glue flowers close to each
other around the ring until covered.

3 With the top wire form still visible, begin
adding another layer of flowers around
the top. The stems should point inward to
the center of the form. Finish gluing flowers
all the way around the form.

4 Trim off excess stems in the center until
neat and even. Remove remnants of glue
threads from hot glue. Cut a length of thick
gold braid to go around the inside of wreath
at least twice. Hot-glue in place to cover the
ends of stems.

5 Tie a piece of gold ribbon to back of
wreath form for hanging. Complete
wreath with a large ribbon bow.

Nature Box

Bring the wonder of nature indoors with this earthy box. Trimmed with painted sticks and acorns, the clay lid is stamped with natural impressions.

what you'll need

Rolling pin
Air-dry clay, such as Crayola Model Magic
Leaves, sticks, evergreens, acorns, or other natural items to make impressions
Cardboard box in desired shape; knife
Thick white crafts glue; paintbrush
Decoupage medium; sand
Acrylic paints in cream, magenta, purple, and green
Brown antiquing gel; rag
Gold highlighting medium, such as Rub 'n' Buff

now make it together

1. Roll out clay as shown in Photo A, *below*, to approximately ¼-inch thick and large enough to cover the box lid. Work quickly because this clay dries very fast.

2. Gently lay the box lid on the clay and trim to the shape of the lid, as shown in Photo B. Remove excess clay and store it in a well-sealed bag.

3. Firmly press leaves and other items into the clay, leaving a good impression, as shown in Photo C. Remove all items. Let the clay dry. With the impression side up, glue the clay piece to the lid. Let it dry.

4. Paint the sides of the box with a coat of decoupage medium. While the decoupage medium is still wet, sprinkle sand on it to add texture. Let it dry.

5. Paint the entire piece cream. Paint the acorns using magenta, purple, and green. Let the paint dry. Cut sticks to fit the lid and box sides as shown, *right*. Paint the sticks as desired. Let the paint dry. Glue the sticks to the lid and the sides of the box. Glue the three acorns in the center of the lid. Let the glue dry.

6. Coat the entire piece with a coat of decoupage medium. Let it dry.

7. Paint a coat of brown antiquing gel over entire surface. Gently wipe the antiquing gel off before it is entirely dry, leaving brown in the crevices to bring out the texture and impressions. Let the antiquing gel dry.

8. Highlight all of the raised areas with a small amount of gold highlighting medium. Let it dry.

Talk With Your Kids
· · · ·
Visit with your kids about respecting nature and conserving our natural resources.

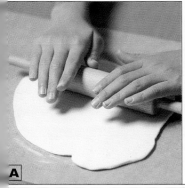

A

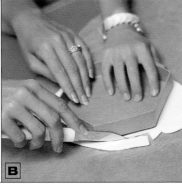

B

C

Beautifully Crumpled Covers

A plain paper grocery sack gives new life as arty photo album or journal cover.

what you'll need

Brown paper bag; scissors; album to cover
Oil pastel sticks
Newspapers; brown shoe polish; paper towel
Gold spray paint; spray adhesive; iron
Dried pressed leaves; raffia
Glossy decoupage medium; paintbrush

now make it together

1 Cut a piece of brown paper bag larger than size of album to be covered. Lay it flat and color the entire surface randomly using oil pastel sticks as shown in Photo A, *below*. Apply color heavily, overlapping if desired.

2 Crumple colored paper with color side inward. Hold under running water as shown in Photo B, squeezing paper until completely soaked. Squeeze out the excess water.

3 Lay wet, wrinkled paper on newspapers. As shown in Photo C, dab a generous amount of shoe polish onto wet, wrinkled paper. Let polish soak into wrinkles. Dab off extra shoe polish with paper towels.

4 Lay wet, wrinkled paper onto newspaper and lightly spray with a mist of gold spray paint from an angle, as shown in Photo D. Spray lightly so the paint does not cover the crevices. Let the paper dry.

5 Cover ironing board. Iron with a cool iron on wrong side, as shown in Photo E, leaving a texture. Apply spray adhesive to the back side of paper and lay on work surface with the sticky side up. Lay album on paper, allowing paper to extend beyond the edges. Trim each side to make neat edge, leaving enough to fold inward. Fold in all edges neatly, using extra adhesive where needed.

6 Paint a coat of glossy decoupage medium over surface of covered album. Let dry.

7 Spray a dried, pressed leaf and a small amount of raffia gold. Let them dry.

8 Apply a generous amount of decoupage medium to area where you want the leaf and raffia placed. Arrange items on the paper. Paint decoupage medium over leaf and raffia until secured. Apply several coats if needed.

A

B

C

D

E

Leaf-Laden Pots

Gather leaves and let their interesting shapes inspire you to make these shimmering flowerpots.

what you'll need

Leaves
Heavy book
Terra-cotta flowerpot
Rubber cement
Burgundy, purple, or other desired colors of
  spray paint

now make it together

1 Choose leaves that have interesting shapes that will fit on the clay pot. To flatten the leaves, place them under a heavy book until dry.

2 Wash and dry flowerpot. Brush rubber cement on one side of leaves as shown *below*. Let it dry. Brush on a second coat. Let it dry to a tacky, but not dry, stage. Position the leaves onto the pot to create a pattern.

3 Spray a light coat of the desired paint color over the entire pot. Spray a second light coat if necessary. Let the paint dry.

4 Peel off the leaves. Rub off any remaining rubber cement from the pot.

19

Bright Idea
••••
Make three or four laundry bags in different colors to sort whites, brights, and dark clothing.

Carry-All Can

As the school year begins, organize yourself with these handy containers that are as pretty as they are practical.

what you'll need

Tall stacked-chip container
Construction paper
Thick white crafts glue
Stickers or paper cutouts
Clear self-adhesive vinyl
Ribbon
Ice pick
2 brad fasteners

now make it together

1 Wrap the container with paper, gluing the ends to the container. Let glue dry.

2 Place stickers or glue cutouts onto paper as desired. Cover the container with vinyl. Wrap and glue ribbon around the top and bottom of the container. Let dry.

3 Poke holes on both sides of the top of the can using an ice pick. Insert brad fasteners into the holes. Tie the ends of the ribbon to the fasteners to create a handle.

Laundry Bag

Keep clothes off the floor with this cheerful laundry bag bursting with playful characters.

what you'll need

Cardboard piece smaller than laundry bag
Fabric laundry bag in a bright color
Fabric paint pens in black and desired colors
Embroidery floss; needle; scissors

now make it together

1 Slip the cardboard piece inside the laundry bag so the paint does not bleed through to the other side. Using the bag, *above*, for ideas, have the kids draw boys and girls, or other motifs, on one side of the laundry bag using a black paint pen. Let it dry.

2 Use colored paint pens to add details to clothing, shoes, and faces as desired. Let the paint dry.

3 Thread desired colors of embroidery floss through a needle. Sew through fabric where bows are desired on the characters. Tie floss into bows and trim the ends. Between figures, sew through fabric with floss and knot on right side.

Talk With Your Kids
····
Have your kids tell you about their best friends— what they like most about each of them.

Back-to-School Necklaces

This clay-bead jewelry is so much fun to make. Personalize a piece for each of your school buddies and favorite relatives.

what you'll need

Alphabet macaroni
Acrylic enamel paints in desired colors
Paintbrush
Oven-bake clay, such as Sculpey, in a variety of colors
Straight pin
Scissors
Beading thread; ruler
Necklace clasps
Seed beads in desired colors

now make it together

1 Decide what message to put on the necklace. Find the corresponding letters of alphabet macaroni. Paint the letters as desired. Let dry.

2 Make small ropes from two colors of clay. Twist together to marbleize. Roll pea-size pinches of marbleized clay into balls. Press a letter into one side of clay ball, flattening slightly. Use a straight pin to make a hole through clay, creating a bead. Bake in the oven according to the clay manufacturer's instructions. Let cool.

3 Cut a piece of thread 5 inches longer than desired necklace length. Tie one half of clasp to an end. Decide how to space the lettered beads with seed beads. String beads on thread. End with the other side of the clasp. Knot and trim thread.

Cool Paper Book Covers

For a great after-school project, decorate paper with different techniques, and then cover your notebooks and textbooks with your creations.

what you'll need

Paper grocery bag; scissors
Thick crayons; watercolor paints
Paper towels
Finger paint
Construction paper
Sponge
Comb
Paintbrush
Corrugated cardboard
Book
Ruler
Tape

batiked paper

now make it together

1 **TO MAKE BATIKED PAPER,** cut a brown paper grocery bag along one fold. Then cut off the bottom and flatten the bag. With thick, light-colored crayons, color geometric designs all over the bag (light, bright colors work the best). Crumple the bag and place it in a bucket of water to create crackle lines. Gently squeeze the bag, lay it flat, and let it dry. Brush dark watercolor paints over the crayon. Blot with paper towels if needed. Let the paint dry.

These photos help show how to make the swirly paper.

swirly paper

2 TO MAKE SWIRLY PAPER,
glob finger paint onto a sheet of construction paper as shown in Photo A, *above*. Spread out paint using a sponge (see Photo B). Use a comb (Photo C), a paintbrush, a piece of cardboard with notches cut into it, or another tool to create patterns on the paper. Let the paint dry.

3 TO MAKE FADED-SHAPES PAPER, lay
construction paper on a patio or porch on a sunny day. Place a variety of objects or cutouts on the paper. Return in a few hours to see what has happened to your paper!

4 TO WRAP YOUR BOOK, lay the paper,
plain side up, on a flat surface. Open the book you want to cover and put it with its spine in the middle of the paper. The paper should be at least 2 inches bigger than the book all the way around.

5 Make a crease along the top of the
book the length of the paper. Make another crease along the bottom of the book. Fold the paper in along both creases as shown in Photos D and E.

6 Keeping the book closed, crease the
paper again along the edges of the book's front and back cover. Fold the paper in along these creases too.

7 Slip the book's front cover into the end
pocket formed by folding the paper. Do the same with the back cover as shown in Photo F. If needed, readjust the creases to get a better fit. Tape the end flaps to the outside paper if desired.

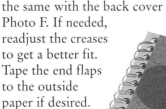

faded-shapes papers

Talk With Your Kids
....
Take turns talking about favorite (and least favorite) school classes, books, and teachers.

These photos show how to wrap your book.

Rockin' Writers

With every move of your hand, these crazy little creatures wiggle and jiggle. The faster you work, the goofier they get.

what you'll need

2 chenille stems
1½-inch wood bead
Scissors
2 small beads
Thumbtack; pencil
Permanent marker

now make it together

1 Fold a chenille stem in half, creating a small loop in the middle. Bring chenille stem ends together. Push wood bead over both ends. Wrap the middle of the second chenille stem below the wood bead to create the creature's arms.

2 Trim about 1 inch off the arms and loop one small bead on either end to form hands. Attach the creature to the pencil by inserting a thumbtack through the small loop at the creature's feet and then pushing the thumbtack into the pencil eraser.

3 Give your creature character by drawing a funny face on the wood bead with a permanent marker.

Beautiful Zootiful Toppers

Tame a lion pen to finish off your ferocious homework, a zebra to gallop through a book report, or an elephant (who never forgets) to make study notes for that big test.

what you'll need

Polymer clay
Ballpoint pen with cap
Pencil

now make it together

1 Form a 1-inch ball out of the clay you choose to create the animal's head. Gently pinch and pull clay to form ears and nose. Add contrasting colors of clay for eyes, tusks, mane, or stripes. Make sure all the pieces you add are firmly attached. Avoid making any thin animal parts because they will burn or crack easily.

2 Carefully push the cap of the pen into the animal head. Leave the cap in the head, but remove the rest of the pen before baking. Insert a pencil into clay-covered pen cap. Bake according to the clay manufacturer's instructions.

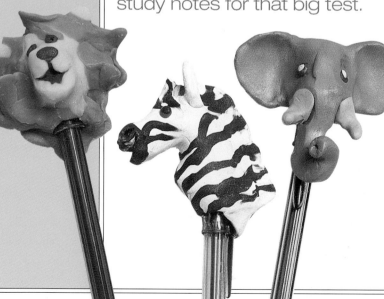

Pencil Mark

Don't skip over a word you don't know—jot it down on this fun bookmark and look up the word later!

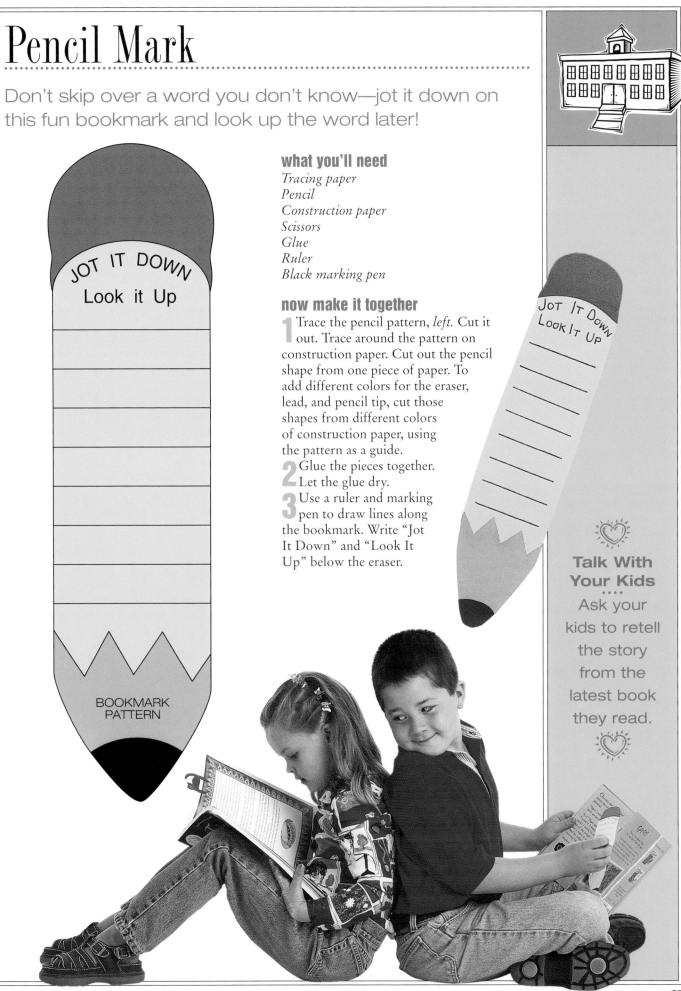

JOT IT DOWN
Look it Up

BOOKMARK
PATTERN

what you'll need
Tracing paper
Pencil
Construction paper
Scissors
Glue
Ruler
Black marking pen

now make it together

1. Trace the pencil pattern, *left.* Cut it out. Trace around the pattern on construction paper. Cut out the pencil shape from one piece of paper. To add different colors for the eraser, lead, and pencil tip, cut those shapes from different colors of construction paper, using the pattern as a guide.

2. Glue the pieces together. Let the glue dry.

3. Use a ruler and marking pen to draw lines along the bookmark. Write "Jot It Down" and "Look It Up" below the eraser.

JOT IT DOWN
LOOK IT UP

Talk With Your Kids
. . . .
Ask your kids to retell the story from the latest book they read.

Pen Pals

Make homework fun with these jazzy pens.

what you'll need

*Embroidery floss
Ruler
Beads; sequins
Tape
Ballpoint pens
Thick white crafts glue
Scissors*

now make it together

1 To make the tail that will hang off the pen's end, tie a knot in a 2½-inch piece of embroidery floss. Thread the floss with beads and sequins.

2 Tape the end of the floss to the pen's end. Cut a 3-foot piece of floss and tape the end to the pen's base near where you taped the tail.

3 Wrap the floss tightly around the pen's barrel. Stop periodically while wrapping and slide beads or sequins onto the floss.

4 When you've covered the entire pen with floss, trim the end and glue it to the last section of wrapped floss.

5 To create pens with bands of color, tape two colors of floss to the end of a pen. Stretch the first color along the pen's barrel. Wrap a few coils of the second color on top of the first color. Now alternate by wrapping a few coils of the first color on top of the second. Alternate as desired.

Wall of Fame

Create a mini gallery for all your best works—from your watercolor art assignment to your A+ essay.

what you'll need

*Scissors
Poster board in desired
   color
Corkboard with wood frame
Ruler
Pencil
Double-sided tape
Glue stick
Colored papers*

now make it together

1 To create the frame, cut out a rectangular center section from poster board that is slightly smaller than the corkboard frame.

2 Stick double-sided tape along the corkboard's wooden frame. Affix the poster board to the tape.

3 Trim the outside edges of the poster board with long curving lines and circular corners, as shown, *above*.

4 Decorate the frame by gluing on paper swirls, circles, stripes, crescent moons, or other desired shapes. Let the glue dry.

Page Critters

You'll never lose your place with these colorful pets marking your page.

what you'll need

Tracing paper; pencil; scissors
Plastic lids from coffee or ice cream
  containers
Paint markers or fabric paint pens

now make it together

1 Trace the desired pattern, *below.* Cut out the shape.

2 Carefully cut off the rim of a plastic lid, leaving only the smooth center. Trace around the pattern on the lid. Cut it out.

3 Use markers or fabric paint to color the plastic and add eyes, a nose, and whiskers to your animal.

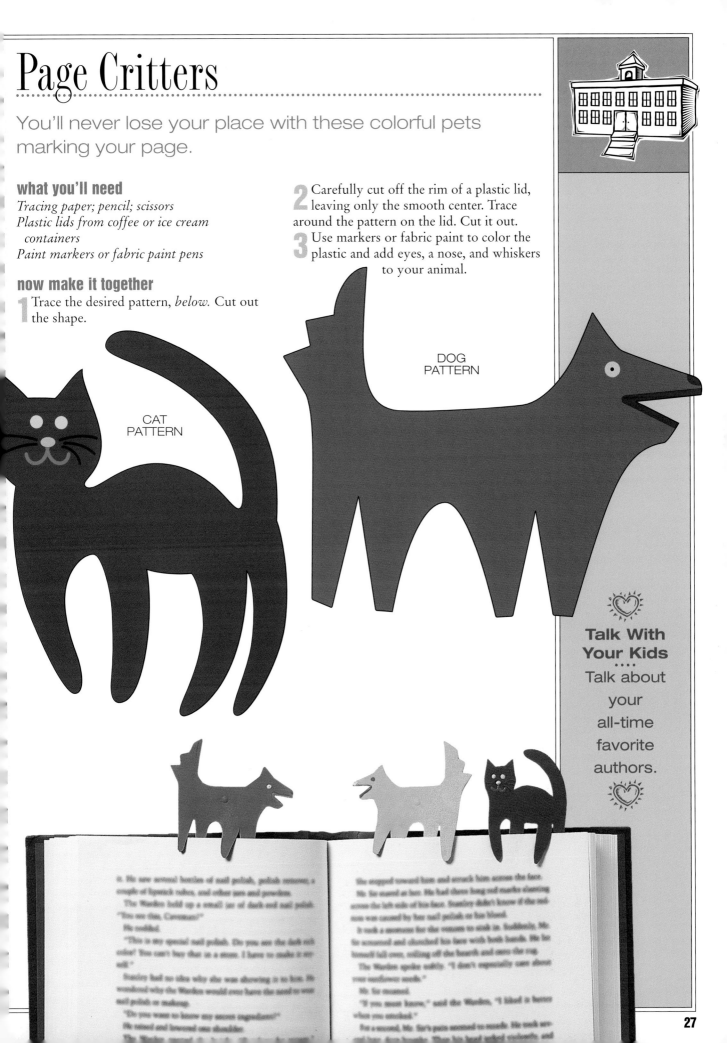

CAT
PATTERN

DOG
PATTERN

**Talk With
Your Kids**
• • • •
Talk about
your
all-time
favorite
authors.

Triple-Deck Bird Feeder

Serve your feathered friends a three-course meal with this tiered feeder made from cake pans.

what you'll need

Safety glasses
5-, 8-, and 10-inch cake pans
Electric drill and bit
7½- and 12-inch stool legs
2-inch wood doll head
Decorative wood finial; wood ornament
Metallic spray paint in two shades each of
 purple and blue
Newspapers; silver marking pen
Metallic acrylic paints in purple and blue
Small flat paintbrush
Double-end dowel screws
Screw eye; silver chain; S hook; pliers
Acrylic sealer

now make it together

1 Mark holes in the center of each cake pan. Wearing safety glasses, drill holes in cake pans and in the ends of each stool leg. Drill a hole in the center of the flat side of the doll head. Drill a hole in the bottom of the finial.

2 In a well-ventilated work area, turn the cake pans upside down on newspapers. Spray-paint the cake pans using light coats of purple and blue paints. Let dry. Continue adding light layers until you achieve a desired look. Spray-paint the wood pieces silver. Let the pieces dry.

3 Use a silver marking pen to draw designs such as swirls, dots, squiggles, and stripes on the painted pans. Let dry.

4 Paint details on wood pieces using blue and purple acrylic paint. Let dry.

5 Connect the pieces using dowel screws between the stool legs, the finial on top, and the wood doll head on the bottom.

6 Add a screw eye in the top of the finial. Attach the chain using an S hook. Attach a screw eye on the bottom of the wood doll head. Using pliers, open the hanger loop for the ornament slightly. Slip the wire hanger loop over the screw eye. Close the loop.

7 Spray the entire bird feeder with acrylic sealer. Let dry.

Talk With Your Kids
····
Grab the binoculars and do some bird-watching in your own backyard. Then check out a library book to learn more about each bird you see.

Cottage Birdhouse

Make your backyard birds a welcoming retreat that's as detailed as a cottage in the mountains.

what you'll need

Tracing paper
Pencil
Scissors
½-inch-thick wood
⅝-inch-thick wood
Saw
Wood glue
Drill; 1-inch and ⅛-inch bits
Small finishing nails; hammer
Two ¾-inch wood screws; screwdriver
Green acrylic paint
Medium flat paintbrush
2 tubes of brown weatherproof caulk
Very fine gravel (available at hobby stores in
   the model railroad supply section)
Wood stain

Rag; weatherproof sealer
Acrylic paint in barn red, black, and light blue
Strips of wood for windows; hacksaw

(continued on page 30)

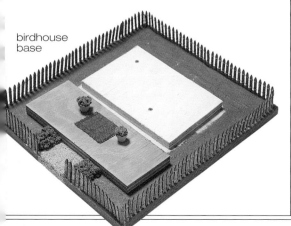

birdhouse
base

Bright Idea
. . . .
Pieces of bark make an interesting birdhouse roof. For this project, cut bark pieces into 1½×1½-inch squares to use in place of cedar shims.

Clear adhesive, such as Liquid Nails
1 package of cedar door shims; stones
Hot-glue gun and hot-glue sticks
2 small clay pots; small scrap of burlap
Green foam moss and mini fencing
 (available at hobby stores in the model
 railroad supply section); fine wire
Waterproof varnish

now make it together

1 Using the patterns, *below and opposite,* as guides, draw pattern pieces on tracing paper. Cut out the pattern pieces and trace onto ½-inch-thick wood. Mark a 14×16-inch rectangle on the ⅝-inch-thick wood for the base.

2 Cut out all pieces. Save sawdust and set aside. Cut out door and glue in place with wood glue on the front panel as shown on pattern. When glue is dry, drill a 1-inch hole through both layers as shown.

3 Assemble the birdhouse as shown in diagram, *opposite,* using small finishing nails. Place the 8⅞×5⅞ house base piece on the birdhouse base as shown, *below.* Drill two small holes and screw the pieces together as shown on *page 29.*

4 For the base, paint the grass area green. Add some fine sawdust into the paint to give it texture. Paint the sides and let dry.

5 Cover sidewalk area with brown caulk, which will also be used for the house. Spread it about ⅛-inch thick. Press fine gravel into brown caulk.

6 Stain the porch board and wipe dry. Brush on weatherproof sealer. Glue porch in place.

7 Paint the trim red around roof. Paint the door red. Cut the pieces for the windows and paint red. Paint the background window areas onto front panel. Paint black first. Before black dries, paint in light blue diagonal streaks for windows. Let dry. Use clear adhesive to glue on window frames.

8 Next add shingles on roof. Cut the cedar shims into 1½-inch-long pieces. Begin gluing onto roof starting on the bottom in front. Glue the first row on side by side. Begin the next row with a ¾-inch-wide piece. Overlap it onto the bottom row about ¼ inch. Finish out the row. Alternate the beginning of each row with ¾-inch-wide and 1½-inch-wide pieces. Overlap each row about ¼ inch. Finish the front side. Do the back side the same way, beginning at the bottom.

9 Begin adding stones to house sides. Spread brown caulk onto sides. Spread it about ¼-inch thick. Press stones into caulk. Arrange according to the shape of the stones. Make sure you leave the bottom ⅞ inch clear on the front panel so it will fit against the porch board.

10 Hot-glue two small clay pots onto porch where shown on *page 29.*

11 Cut a small rug out of a piece of burlap. Paint stripes or a plaid pattern and paint fringed ends with acrylic paints. Let dry. Glue the rug to the porch board.

12 Soak the green foam in waterproof varnish. Fill the pots. Spread adhesive in bush area. Place small bits of foam on adhesive to resemble bushes.

13 Nail small finishing nails in all four corners and one on each side of the sidewalk. Attach fence around outside. Use adhesive or very fine wire to anchor fence to nails.

14 Set the birdhouse on the base. For cleaning, simply lift off.

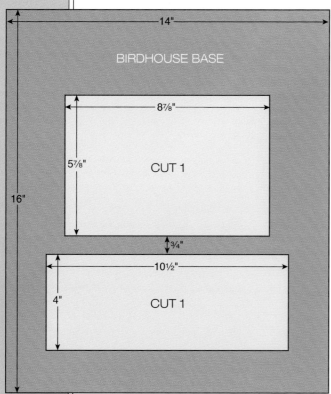
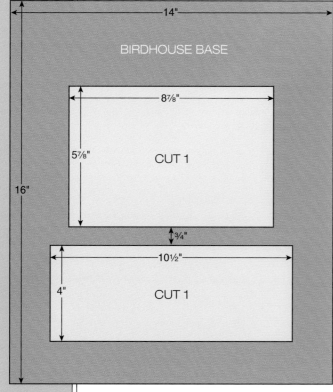

14"
BIRDHOUSE BASE
8⅞"
5⅞"
CUT 1
16"
¾"
10½"
4"
CUT 1

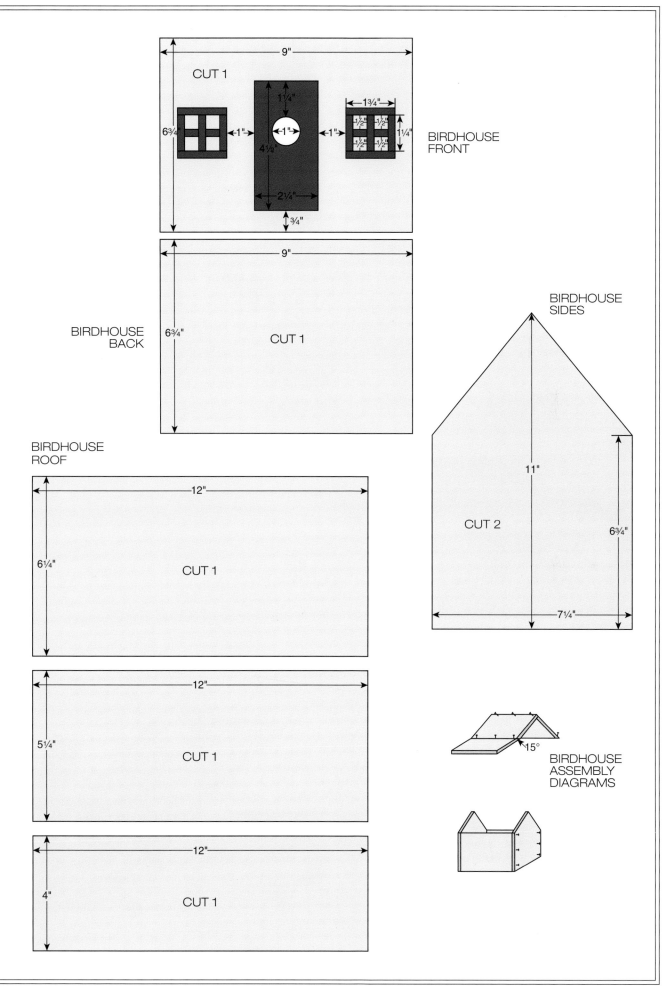

CUT 1

BIRDHOUSE
FRONT

9"

6¾"

1¼"

1"

1"

1¾"

½" ½"

½" ½"

1¼"

4½"

2¼"

¾"

BIRDHOUSE
BACK

9"

6¾"

CUT 1

BIRDHOUSE
SIDES

CUT 2

11"

6¾"

7¼"

BIRDHOUSE
ROOF

12"

6¼"

CUT 1

12"

5¼"

CUT 1

12"

4"

CUT 1

15°

BIRDHOUSE
ASSEMBLY
DIAGRAMS

Party Time Tableware and Napkin Rings

Cheer on your sports teams with plasticware and napkin rings that display their colors and go-team-go sentiments.

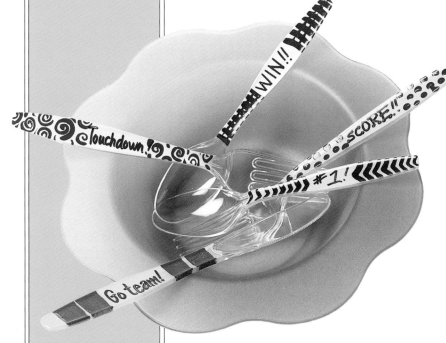

Party Time Silverware

what you'll need

Acrylic enamel paints
Fine paintbrush
Plastic silverware

now make it together

1 Using your team's colors, paint the handle portion of the utensil, leaving the center open for a message if desired. Paint stripes, dots, zigzags, swirls, or any other desired design. Let dry.

2 Paint a message in the center of the handle if desired. Let the paint dry.

Note: If reusing the tableware, wash it gently in warm water. Do not soak or put into a dishwasher.

Party Time Napkin Rings

what you'll need

Chenille stems in team colors
Scissors; ruler
Wood beads in team colors
Paper napkins

now make it together

1 Cut chenille stems to measure approximately 10 inches.

2 Twist ends of chenille stems together, leaving 1½-inch tails.

3 Thread beads in team colors onto ends of chenille stems.

Bend the ends of the stems to prevent the beads from slipping off.

4 Roll up a paper napkin. Slide into the napkin ring. Shape the ends of the beaded chenille stems as desired.

Bright Idea
••••
Practice rhyming words by making up team cheers.

**Talk With
Your Kids**
....
Talk about
being a
good sport
and what
makes an
outstanding
athlete.

High-Flying
Party Pennants

Encourage a team or a teammate
with these clever pennants.

what you'll need
Crafting foam
Construction paper
Stencils
Scissors
Thick white crafts glue
Paper punch
Dowel

now make it together

1 Cut triangle shapes from crafting foam
or construction paper.

2 Using stencils, cut letters and numbers.
Cut additional shapes such as circles,
squares, stripes, stars, and triangles.

3 Glue the shapes to the pennants with
thick crafts glue. Let the glue dry.

4 Punch four holes along the short side of
each pennant using a paper punch. Weave
a dowel through the holes.

Colorful Pumpkin Wands

Add Halloween fun to your landscaping with these pumpkins-on-a-stick that you make in just a couple of quick steps.

what you'll need
*Driftwood or other sticks 2 to 3 feet long
(gathering your sticks can be a fun family
outing!)
Acrylic paints in orange, purple, lime green,
and black
Paintbrush
2-inch-long threaded nails
Hammer
Wire cutters
Safety glasses
Small pumpkins*

now make it together
1 Paint stripes or other designs on the sticks. Let the paint dry. Paint the pumpkin stems a solid color. Let dry.

2 Carefully hammer a nail into the end of the stick. Put on safety glasses. Use wire cutters to snip off the head of the nail. Push the bottom of the pumpkin onto the nail.

Bright Idea
····
For a no-carve jack-o'-lantern, draw a face on a pumpkin using black paint pen. Let dry. Fill in the drawn areas with yellow paint pen to resemble candlelight shining through.

Spellbound Pumpkin

Decorate a spooktacular pumpkin with words made from alphabet macaroni.

what you'll need
*Pumpkin; alphabet macaroni
Paintbrush; glossy decoupage medium
Acrylic metallic paints in copper, green,
purple, gold, or other desired colors
Pencil with round-tip eraser*

now make it together
1 Decide what words or phrases to add to the pumpkin. Find those macaroni letters. On the pumpkin, paint a ⅛-inch line of decoupage medium where you want the words. Place the letters on the decoupage medium. Let it dry.

2 Paint the top surfaces of the letters lightly, using metallic paint. Use only one color on the entire word or phrase so it stands out as a unit. Let the paint dry.

3 To make dots, dip the eraser end of the pencil into copper paint. Carefully dot the paint onto the pumpkin where desired. Let dry.

Laced-Up-Tight Pumpkin

Colorful plastic-coated wires thread easily through the predrilled holes in this bright orange pumpkin.

what you'll need

Knife
Pumpkin
Spoon
Hand drill with ³/₁₆-inch bit
Plastic-coated wire in white, green, purple,
  yellow, orange, blue, and red
Wire cutters

now make it together

1 Cut a circle around the stem of the pumpkin. Remove the stem and scoop out the insides.

2 Using a hand drill, make horizontal pairs of holes on each side of pumpkin seams, approximately ¾ inch apart. Start just below the top of the pumpkin. Drill as many sets as necessary to reach the bottom, making a pair of holes approximately every inch. Continue drilling until the entire pumpkin is drilled.

3 Bend the end of a piece of wire, shaping it into a U. Poke straight end of wire through the top hole on the inside of the pumpkin. Push the bent end into the pumpkin to secure. Poke wire back to inside, using the hole one over and one

down to create a diagonal line. Continue in this manner, adding wire when necessary. To create the X, reverse the lacing order.

4 Trim excess from wires, leaving 1 inch at the end to bend over and push into inside of pumpkin.

Bright Idea
••••
For someone special with an autumn birthday, make this pumpkin. Then drill small holes in the top. Place birthday candles in the holes for a fun Happy Birthday surprise.

Carnival Pumpkin

You'll have to get your fingers wet to leave your mark on this colorful pumpkin!

what you'll need
Pumpkin
Newspapers
Acrylic enamel paints in bright colors
Flat paintbrush

now make it together

1 Wash and dry the pumpkin. Cover the work surface with newspapers.

2 Paint a wide zigzag stripe around the middle of the pumpkin. Paint wide stripes from the bottom of the zigzag to the bottom of the pumpkin. Use a flat paintbrush to paint small squares on the top of the pumpkin. Let the paint dry.

3 Use your finger to add dots to the zigzag stripe. Let the paint dry.

Snowman Pumpkin

This merry, not scary, character may last until the first snow falls.

what you'll need

Large and small pumpkins
Two 3-inch-long nails
Safety glasses
Wire cutters
Black permanent marker
Wood plug or button
Ribbon and trim for hat
Small black felt hat
Hot-glue gun and hot-glue sticks
Rectangular piece of fabric for scarf
Colored rickrack
1 small, 2 medium, and 2 large wood stars
*Acrylic paints in yellow, orange, lime green,
  black, dark orange, and purple*
Paintbrush
Dried leaves
Sticks

now make it together

1 Choose two pumpkins that will stack well together to make a shape like a snowman. Break the stem off the larger pumpkin. Pound two nails halfway into the top of the large pumpkin. Wearing safety glasses, clip off the nail heads with a wire cutter. Press the smaller pumpkin down onto the nails. Draw a face on the pumpkin with a black permanent marker.

2 Use a button or wood plug painted dark orange for the nose. Glue on with hot glue. Add ribbon and trim to the purchased hat with glue. Tie a rectangular strip of fabric around the neck. Glue on colored rickrack for trim.

3 Paint the small and medium wood stars yellow. Paint the large stars lime green. Brush a very small amount of orange in the points of the yellow stars. Paint the edges of the medium yellow stars black. Add two small black dots to the center of each yellow star by dipping the handle end of paintbrush into paint and dotting onto surface. Let dry.

4 Glue the medium stars onto the large stars to make buttons. Glue the small star on the hat and the layered stars on the snowman's belly.

5 Paint the leaves using acrylic paint. Let dry. Pierce holes in the sides of the large pumpkin for arms. Insert small sticks into holes. Hot-glue the painted leaves onto the sticks.

**Talk With
Your Kids**
....
Explain
the four
seasons of
the year
and the
changes
that relate
to each.

37

Bright Idea
····
If you desire a more natural look, use this same technique using twine and jute.

Floss-Wrapped Pumpkin

Share sewing basics with these striped pumpkins wrapped with bands of embroidery floss.

what you'll need

Knife; pumpkin
Spoon
Paring knife
Cotton embroidery floss; needle

now make it together

1 Cut a circle around the stem of the pumpkin. Remove the stem and scoop out the insides.

2 Use a paring knife to cut narrow vertical slits around pumpkin, approximately every 2 inches. Remove cutouts.

3 To wrap pumpkin sections with floss, first unwind a skein of floss. The entire skein will be used for one wrap. Bring the floss ends together. Double again so you have 4 strands. Thread the folded ends through needle and slide needle to opposite end.

4 From the inside, push the needle through the pumpkin, holding the folded ends on the inside. Bring the floss around a section and push back through the pumpkin and through the folded floss ends to secure. Continue winding the floss around until the entire pumpkin section is covered. Knot floss on the inside. Change floss colors and repeat until all sections are covered with floss.

5 Wrap the stem with floss, securing as on pumpkin wraps. Leave spaces between the wraps if desired. The floss on the pumpkin wraps can also be separated if desired to create horizontal lines.

Black Cat Pumpkin

All dressed up for Halloween, this black cat is made from two stacked pumpkins.

what you'll need
Small round pumpkin; large tall pumpkin
Sharp knife; spoon
Black spray paint
Flat toothpicks; hot-glue gun; hot-glue sticks
2 flat, green marbles
Ice pick
White crafting wire
Black chenille stems
Candle
Fabric or tie

now make it together

1 Cut the stem out of the small pumpkin, cutting the circle about 1½ inches from the stem. Scoop out the insides. Using the photo, *below,* for inspiration, cut two eyes high enough to fit the marbles. Cut out the nose and mouth. Cut two ear shapes from the pumpkin skin around the stem. Cut the stem off the large pumpkin without cutting through the pumpkin skin.

2 In a well-ventilated work area, spray-paint the pumpkins and the ear shapes black. Do not spray directly into the openings for the cat's eyes, mouth, and nose.

3 Hot-glue the marbles to the wide ends of toothpicks. Let dry. Push two toothpicks into the bottoms of the ear shapes.

4 Push the ears into place on the head. Push the marble eyes into place.

5 Use an ice pick to poke three holes on each side of the nose opening for whiskers. Cut six 6-inch-long pieces of wire for whiskers. Shape wires as desired. Poke one end of each wire into the holes made next to the nose.

6 Twist together chenille stems to make a tail. Set the tail under the large pumpkin.

7 Place a candle on top of the large pumpkin. Place the head over the candle. Tie a fabric strip or necktie around the cat's neck.

39

**Bright
Idea**
····
Have the
kids draw
jack-o'-
lantern
faces on
paper; then
transfer
them to the
pumpkins
before
carving.

Jolly Jack-o'-Lanterns

These snuggling pals will make you giggle right along
with them.

what you'll need

3 pumpkins approximately the same size
Carving knife; spoon; candles

now make it together

1 Trim off one side of each of the outer
pumpkins so they can sit close together.
Cut the bottom off the center pumpkin.

2 Scoop out the insides of the pumpkins.
Carve desired faces on the pumpkins.
3 Place candles in each of the pumpkins.
Light the candles.

*Note: For safety, do not leave burning
candles unattended.*

Beaded Pumpkin

Kids of all ages will love to help add polka dots to this pumpkin-patch beauty.

what you'll need

Small pumpkin
White thumbtacks
White map pins
Colored quilting pins
Pony beads in orange, yellow, black,
  and purple

now make it together

1 Wash the pumpkin and let it dry. Trim the stem straight if necessary.

2 Randomly push thumbtacks and map pins into pumpkin. To attach a bead, place a bead on a quilting pin; then push it into the pumpkin. Continue adding beads until you have the desired look.

Talk With Your Kids
• • • •
Talk about keeping the work area tidy while crafting. When doing this project, be sure to work over a box lid or baking dish to avoid having sharp pins and tacks landing on the floor.

Spooky Surprise

This friendly ghost, peeking from his pumpkin home, is fun to make from lightweight clay. With a few bright details, this clever pumpkin becomes the center of attention at your Halloween party.

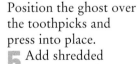
Small pumpkin
Knife; spoon
Four 8-inch-long pieces of ¼-inch dowel
Pencil sharpener
Acrylic paints in lime green and purple
Paintbrush
White air-dry clay, such as Crayola Model Magic clay
2 small black beads; 1 large black bead
Toothpicks
Shredded colored paper

now make it together

1 Cut the pumpkin in half horizontally, keeping the cut line as smooth as possible. Clean out the inside by scraping it with a spoon.

2 Sharpen both ends of the dowels in a pencil sharpener for easy insertion into the pumpkin. Paint two dowel pieces lime green and the remaining two purple. Let the paint dry. Add dots on each dowel by dipping the handle of the paintbrush into paint and dotting onto the dowel surfaces. Let the paint dry. Paint the pumpkin stem purple. Let dry. Add green dots. Let dry. Insert the dowels into the bottom half of the pumpkin; then place the pumpkin top on by firmly pressing it onto the dowels.

3 To create the ghost, take a portion of clay suitable for the size of your pumpkin. Knead the clay until it is smooth. Shape the clay into a smooth, oblong piece. Gently twist the top portion to create a ghostly head. Shape arms from small pieces of clay. Position the arms on the ghost's body and press into place. Form the bottom of the ghost to fit inside the pumpkin.

4 Use the photograph, *below*, as a guide to make the eyes and mouth. Press the black beads into the face using a toothpick. Press toothpicks into the bottom of the pumpkin. Position the ghost over the toothpicks and press into place.

5 Add shredded paper around the pumpkin.

Dressed-Up Pumpkins

Create one-of-a-kind no-carve pumpkin people with a variety of items from around the house.

what you'll need

FOR THE GLAMOUR GIRL
Pumpkin
Artificial eyelashes; straw hat; ribbon
Silk flowers
Red raffia
Acrylic paints in red and pink; paintbrush
Thick white crafts glue

FOR THE COWBOY
Pumpkin
Orange foam ball
Scissors
Thick white crafts glue
Cowboy hat; 2 bandannas
Acrylic paints in black, white, and yellow
Paintbrush
Toy sheriff's badge

FOR THE VEGGIE LADY
Pumpkin
Quilting pins
Lettuce
Sweet red peppers
Black olives
Yellow peppers
Hot-glue gun and hot-glue sticks
Thread; needle

now make it together

1 Wash the pumpkin. Let it dry. Trim the stem short if necessary.

2 FOR THE GLAMOUR GIRL, remove backing from artificial eyelashes. Apply to pumpkin, slightly above the center. Use acrylic paints to add a nose, cheeks, and a mouth. Let the paint dry. Glue raffia to the inside of the hat to resemble hair. Glue a ribbon around the hat. Add silk flowers. Set the hat on top of the pumpkin.

3 FOR THE COWBOY, cut a foam ball in half. Glue the flat side of one half to the center of the pumpkin. Using the photo, *above*, as inspiration, paint eyes and a mouth. Let the paint dry. Add a white highlight to the nose and eyes. Tie a bandanna around the cowboy hat. Place on the top of the pumpkin. Tie the remaining bandanna around the bottom of the pumpkin. Secure with a sheriff's badge.

4 FOR THE VEGGIE LADY, pin lettuce on top of the pumpkin for hair. Add olive eyes, a yellow pepper nose, and sweet red pepper ears and mouth. Add yellow pepper earrings. Glue in place using hot glue. For a necklace, string olives on thread.

Bright Idea
••••
Keep an eye on the recycling bin for cans without ridges. You can make mini versions of this treat can to give to friends and neighbors at Halloween time.

Winking Paint Pail

A perfect size for trick-or-treating, this brand-new empty paint can shines with bright enamel paints.

what you'll need

Printer paper; pencil
Scissors; double-sided tape; paint can
Black permanent marking pen
Large rubber band to go around paint can
Acrylic enamel paints in white, black, orange,
  yellow, green, and purple
Paintbrush
Pencil with round-tip eraser

now make it together

1 Trace the pattern, *opposite*, onto printer paper. Cut out the pattern, including the eyes, nose, and mouth. Use small pieces of double-sided tape to place it centered on the front of the paint can.

2 Trace around the pattern with a black permanent marking pen as shown in Photo A, *opposite*.

3 Place the rubber band around the paint can, 1 inch from the bottom. Straighten if necessary to make a straight line. Trace line with marker. Move rubber band 1 inch from the top of the can and draw a second line. Remove the rubber band.

4 Using the drawn lines as guides, paint the top and bottom bands white. Let the paint dry. To make polka dots on the top band as shown in Photo B, *below,* dip the eraser end of a pencil into black paint and dot onto the surface of the paint can. Paint

alternating black checks on the bottom band as shown in Photo C. Let the paint dry.

5 Paint the orange and yellow areas of the pumpkin. Let it dry. Paint swirls, zigzags, and dots in the background as desired. Add green dots inside the black dots on the top band using the handle of a paintbrush dipped into paint. Let dry.

6 Outline the pumpkin details using black paint. Let it dry.

WINKING
PAINT PAIL
PATTERN

Talk With Your Kids
• • • •
Reminisce about your favorite Halloween memories— trick-or-treating, treats you looked forward to, and the costumes you remember.

A

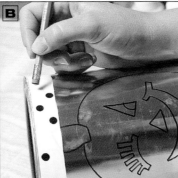

B

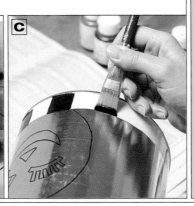

C

Treat-filled Pouches

Surprise family and friends with these clever pouches made from foam and held together with tiny round eyelets.

what you'll need

Tracing paper; pencil
Crafting foam in yellow, orange, white, and purple
Scissors and pinking shears, if desired
Awl
Eyelets and an eyelet tool
Black permanent marker

Bright Idea
· · · ·
For fun Halloween party invitations, make these pouches from colored papers and slip the party information inside.

PUMPKIN
POUCH
PATTERN

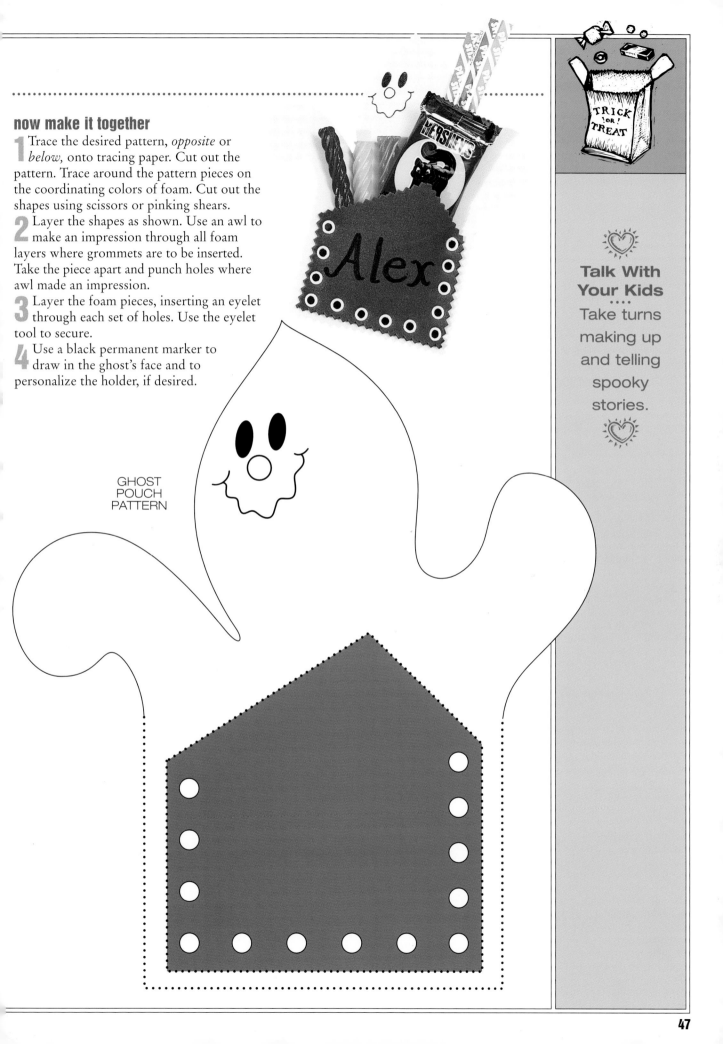

now make it together

1 Trace the desired pattern, *opposite* or *below*, onto tracing paper. Cut out the pattern. Trace around the pattern pieces on the coordinating colors of foam. Cut out the shapes using scissors or pinking shears.

2 Layer the shapes as shown. Use an awl to make an impression through all foam layers where grommets are to be inserted. Take the piece apart and punch holes where awl made an impression.

3 Layer the foam pieces, inserting an eyelet through each set of holes. Use the eyelet tool to secure.

4 Use a black permanent marker to draw in the ghost's face and to personalize the holder, if desired.

GHOST POUCH PATTERN

Talk With Your Kids
• • • •
Take turns making up and telling spooky stories.

47

Ooky 'n' Spooky Treat Cups

A bewitching blend of sweet surprises will satisfy anyone's cravings for a snack. These painted cups are just right to hold a generous portion. Flat glass marbles add dimension to the cat's eyes and spider's body.

what you'll need

Clear plastic punch cups
Tracing paper
Pencil; scissors
Tape
Glass paints in black, green, yellow, and white
Paintbrush
Flat glass marbles in iridescent black and frosted clear or pale green
Silicone glue

OOKY THE CAT PATTERN

now make it together

1 Wash and dry the cups. Avoid touching the areas to be painted.

2 If painting the cat, trace the pattern, *left*, onto tracing paper. Cut out slightly beyond the drawn lines. Tape the pattern to the inside of the cup where you wish to paint the design. Place it low on the cup so the weight of the eyes does not tip the cup.

3 **TO MAKE THE CAT CUP,** paint the cat black. Let the paint dry. Using the pattern as a guide, paint the nose, mouth, and whisker details. To paint the marble eyes, mix a drop of green and yellow. Paint long ovals on the front sides of two frosted marbles. Let dry. Paint smaller black ovals inside the green ones. Let dry. Glue the eyes in place and let dry. Remove the patterns.

4 **TO MAKE THE SPIDER,** glue two iridescent black marbles on the cup. Place them low enough so the cup does not tip. Let the glue dry. Paint on black legs. Let the paint dry.

Candy Corn Bag

This cute bag is as much of a treat as the candies inside.

what you'll need

Tracing paper
Pencil
Felt in white, yellow, orange, and purple
Thick white crafts glue
Pinking shears
Scissors
Acrylic paints in black, white, yellow, and
*   orange*
Paintbrush
Paper bag with handles

now make it together

1 Trace the candy corn pattern, *below.* Cut out. Use pattern to cut one shape from white. Cut a separate tip from white, a center piece from orange, and an end from yellow. Glue these three pieces on the white shape. Let dry.

2 Using pinking shears, cut a rectangle from purple felt, 1 inch smaller than front of bag. Glue to bag front. Center and glue candy corn to purple felt. Let dry.

3 Use paints to add designs to candy corn and purple background. To make large dots, dip the eraser end of a pencil into paint and dot onto the surface. To make small dots, use the handle of a paintbrush. Let the paint dry.

4 Use pinking shears to cut 8-inch-long narrow strips from felts. Tie at the top of the bag handles for a bow.

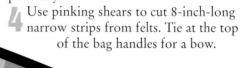

CANDY CORN
PATTERN

Playful Tiger

Catch this playful tiger by the tail, then put some candy in his pail.

what you'll need
Scissors
Furry felt in black and white
Thick white crafts glue
Orange hooded sweat suit
Rope or cording; yardstick
Black tights or a long black sock
Thread; plastic pail
2 orange socks, orange fabric
Face paints in orange, white, and black

now make it together

1 Cut tiger stripes from furry black felt and glue them to an orange hooded sweat suit. Cut an oval of furry white felt and glue it to the front of the shirt. Glue small pieces of white felt to the sides of the hood for cheeks and ears.

2 Cover 2 to 3 feet of rope or cording with one leg of black tights or a long black sock. Sew it to the back of the sweatpants.

3 Glue white felt circles onto socks to make paws.

4 Make a matching treat bucket by covering a plastic pail with orange material and gluing on black stripes.

To PAINT A TIGER FACE, use washable costume makeup in orange, black, and white. Make sure the child's face is clean and dry. Start with white, painting down the middle of the face, around the mouth, and adding a small circle on the chin as shown in Photo A, *left*. Add orange stripes as shown in Photo B. Start just above the eyebrows, using the eyebrows as your guide. Fill in with black stripes. Cover the tip of the nose with black. Draw a black line from the bottom of the nose to the upper lip and add whisker dots in the white area. For the tiger's smile, draw with black just above the child's lips.

Clarise the Clown

Bright fabrics and rickrack turn an ordinary sweat suit into circus attire.

what you'll need
Pencil; ruler
Fusible web paper
Assorted bright solid and polka-dot fabric
Scissors
Blue sweat suit
Thread
Needle
4×72-inch piece of bright fabric
5×72-inch piece of coordinating bright fabric
2 yards each of jumbo rickrack in two colors
1 yard of ⅜-inch-wide grosgrain ribbon
Purchased wig
Hairbands for cuffs
Face paints

now make it together
1 Draw 4- and 5-inch-diameter circles onto web paper. Fuse to assorted bright fabrics. Cut out the fabric pieces and fuse to the sweatshirt and the sweatpants.

2 To make the collar, stitch a narrow hem on two short ends and one long side of each bright fabric rectangle. Topstitch rickrack to each of the long hemmed edges. Layer the narrow strip on top of the wide strip with the right sides facing up. Stitch the raw edges together using a ¼-inch seam allowance. Press the seam open.

3 Gather along the seam to about 18 inches. Stitch the gathered edge onto the grosgrain ribbon. Tie the collar around the neck.

4 Put on wig. Place hairbands around wrists. Paint face as desired.

Talk With Your Kids
····
Talk about clown costumes and circus performers.

LuLu Ladybug

Here's a last-minute costume that will transform any little munchkin into a fun-loving lulu of a ladybug.

what you'll need

Pencil; tracing paper; scissors; paper punch
¼-inch-thick red crafting foam
Thin black crafting foam
Hot-glue gun and hot-glue sticks
4 eyelets and eyelet tool
Pair of black 42-inch-long shoelaces
Purchased red hat and black gloves
Black chenille stem; 2 large, black pom-poms

now make it together

1 Enlarge and trace the wing pattern, *below right*, onto tracing paper. Cut out. Trace the dot pattern and cut out. Cut two wings from red foam and six dots from black foam.

2 Using the diagram, *below left*, glue the short flat edges of the wings together. Glue three dots on each wing. Let dry.

3 Use a paper punch to make two holes at the top of each wing. For reinforcement, add an eyelet to each hole.

4 Tie the shoelaces together at one end. Place the knot by the seam on the wrong side of the wings. Thread the laces through the holes in each wing. To wear, bring laces over the shoulders, criss-cross in the front, and tie at the back waist.

5 For hat, poke a chenille stem through the top of the hat. Glue a pom-pom on each chenille stem end. Let dry.

Bright Idea
····
Use felt for this project if desired. To make it sturdy, glue the wing pieces to medium-weight cardboard.

LADYBUG PLACEMENT DIAGRAM

WING PATTERN (CUT 2)

DOT PATTERN (CUT 6)

LADYBUG PATTERN

1 SQUARE = 1 INCH

Crazy Caterpillar

Kids will inch along in this cozy, comfy costume.

what you'll need

Paper; pencil; tape measure; scissors
2½ yards of 72-inch-wide lime
* green felt*
Large yellow buttons sewing needle
Thread; ½ yard of 72-inch-wide black felt
Thick white crafts glue; ½ yard of
* 72-inch-wide each of pink and yellow felt*
Pinking shears; tracing paper; headband
Metallic chenille stems
2 large pom-poms; black sweats suits
White shoes; green baseball hats; gloves

now make it together

1 Use paper to make an oval arm opening pattern, 12 inches high and 6 inches wide. Make a circular 6-inch-diameter neck opening pattern.

2 Fold green felt in half lengthwise as shown in the diagram, right. Use the patterns to start marking the neck holes 4 inches from the front end at the fold. Leaving 18 inches between neck holes, mark the remaining three neck holes. Cut out the four neck holes.

3 For each arm opening, trace around the pattern 4 inches from the neck opening. Cut out the eight arm holes.

4 Cut scallops across bottom from centers of armholes ash shown in the diagram. Cut front into a vest shape and angle the back to create the look of a tail.

5 Overlap front vest pieces and secure by sewing on large buttons. Stitch back seam.

6 Cut eight 4×24-inch strips from black felt. Glue strips below armholes, trimming to match the bottom scallop.

7 Cut six 8½-inch circles from pink felt using pinking shears. Enlarge and trace the pattern, below. Use the pattern to cut six shapes from yellow felt using scissors. Glue the cutouts as shown, *above*.

8 For antennae, wrap chenille stems around a headband. Glue pom-poms to ends of two stems and wrap around sides of headband. Place over the hat of the leader.

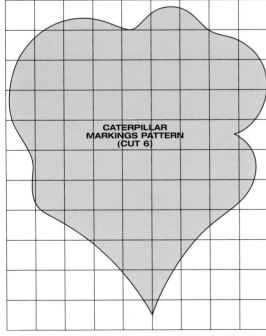

CATERPILLAR
MARKINGS PATTERN
(CUT 6)

CATERPILLAR
PATTERN   1 SQUARE = 1 INCH

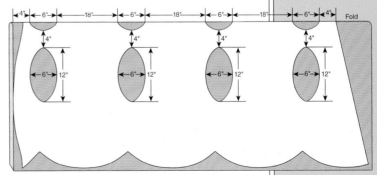

CATERPILLAR DIAGRAM

Talk With Your Kids
. . . .
Research the life stages of a caterpillar and other insects.

Haunting Hands

Scare 'em silly with these quick hand disguises that will have you cackling in no time.

Bright Idea
....
For a fun treat pouch, attach a string strap to cuff of glove. Fill with treats for a special friend.

Monster Hands

what you'll need

An inexpensive pair of work gloves
Scissors; fake fur
Construction paper
School glue
Clothespins
Glitter glue

now make it together

1 Use the gloves as a guide to cut pieces of fur that will cover the back of your hand. Then glue each piece to the back of a glove. Cut small rectangles of fur to glue to the base of each finger on the gloves. Cut out 10 pointed claws from construction paper and glue them to the fingertips. Clamp them with clothespins while the glue dries. After the glue has dried, remove the clamps and apply a coat of glitter glue to each claw.

Witch Hands

what you'll need

An inexpensive pair of green garden gloves
White air-dry clay, such as Crayola Model Magic clay
Washable paint; paintbrush
Construction paper
School glue; scissors
Clothespins
Glitter glue

now make it together

1 Roll about 20 various-size warts out of white clay, pressing the warts gently against a table to flatten one side. After they've dried, paint them a bright color. While the paint is drying, cut out 10 fingernails from construction paper. Glue the nails to the fingertips of the gloves. Clamp them with clothespins while the glue dries. Glue the painted warts to the gloves and let dry. Apply a coat of glitter to the fingernails if desired.

Egg Carton Disguises

You'll be surprised how many people you can fool with these silly faces made from egg cartons!

what you'll need

Clean egg cartons
Scissors
Paints or marking pens in desired colors
Paper punch
Ribbon or shoelace

now make it together

1 Before you start, be sure there is no sign of dirt or broken eggs on the carton. If you use a plastic foam carton, first wash it in soapy water. For a paper carton, place it in a microwave oven on high for 15 seconds.

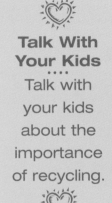

Talk With Your Kids
· · · ·
Talk with your kids about the importance of recycling.

2 With an adult's help, cut the carton into the shapes shown in photos, *above,* or create shapes of your own. Holding the mask away from your face, cut holes for the eyes. Make sure the holes are big enough to see through.

3 Use paints or markers to add designs to the mask. Let it dry.

4 Punch holes at the sides. Insert a shoelace or ribbon into each hole, knotting at the end to secure. Tie the ribbons or laces together to fasten the mask.

Running Wild Masks

Go wild—as a wise owl or rascally raccoon—with these paper-plate masks that are a hoot to make.

what you'll need

Construction paper in black, brown, orange, yellow, light gray, and brown
Elastic cord; 4 beads or buttons
White glue; scissors; paper plates

now make it together

1 To Make the Owl, cut out mask shape from paper plate as shown in Photo A, *below.* Enlarge and trace patterns, *opposite.* Cut orange ears, orange and yellow feathers, black and brown eyes, and orange beak. Cut several 1-inch slits into each piece (except ears and beak) for a feathery look as in Photo B. Glue ears behind plate. Layer and glue feathers to front of mask as shown in Photo C. Fold and glue beak to front. Glue eye pieces in place. Cut eye holes in plate. Poke small holes on either side of mask. Pull elastic cord through holes and tie to button or bead to prevent knot from pulling through. Cut eye holes with scissors.

2 To Make the Raccoon, cut the paper plate as for the owl. Enlarge and trace the patterns, *opposite.* Cut a bandit mask and ears from brown. Tear pieces of paper for "fur." Glue ears to plate. Layer and glue fur pieces front and back. Glue eyes, nose, and paper whiskers to mask. Poke small holes on either side of mask. Pull elastic cord through holes and tie to button or bead to prevent knot from pulling through. Cut eye holes with scissors.

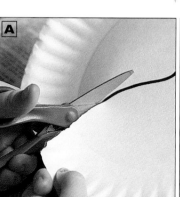

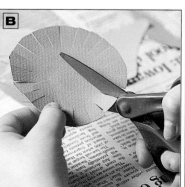

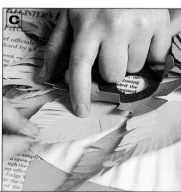

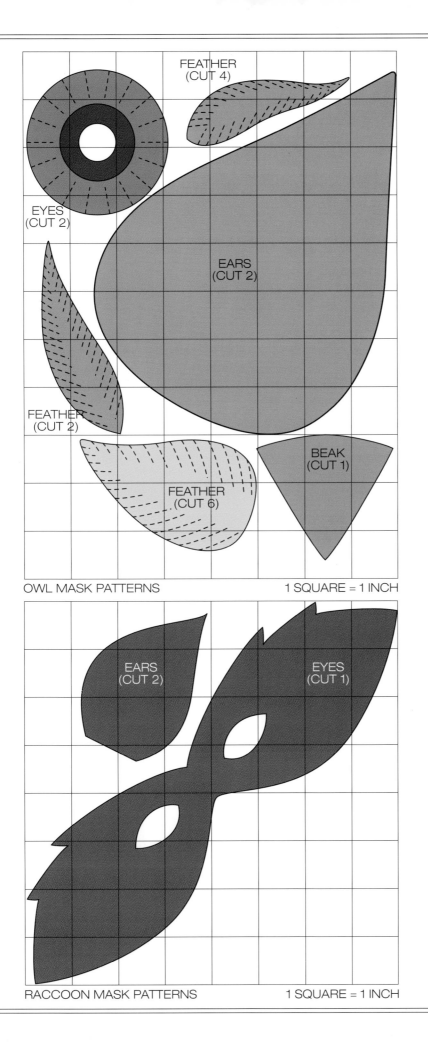

FEATHER
(CUT 4)

EYES
(CUT 2)

EARS
(CUT 2)

FEATHER
(CUT 2)

FEATHER
(CUT 6)

BEAK
(CUT 1)

OWL MASK PATTERNS   1 SQUARE = 1 INCH

EARS
(CUT 2)

EYES
(CUT 1)

RACCOON MASK PATTERNS   1 SQUARE = 1 INCH

**Talk With
Your Kids**
• • • •
Discuss wild
animals and
ways to
help protect
our nature
friends.

57

Bright Idea
····
Make a mini wig for your little one's dolly so they can play dress-up together.

Family Disguises

You'll have everyone guessing who you are this Halloween with these fun disguises that are a breeze to make.

Goldie Locks

what you'll need

Plastic headband; scissors; yellow yarn
Thick white crafts glue; yardstick
2 yards of 1-inch-wide plaid ribbon

now make it together

1 Cut approximately 48 nine-inch lengths of yarn for bangs. Working with two strands at a time, fold in half. Place the loop under the center of the headband. Thread the yarn ends through the loop and pull tight. Continue working on both sides of the first yarn until bang area is completed. Dab glue under the yarn at both ends to hold in place.

2 For ponytails, cut approximately 100 three-foot lengths of yarn. With ends even, tie a piece of yarn tightly in the center; then tie around center of headband.

3 Cut the ribbon into four equal lengths. Using a pair of ribbons, tie around long lengths of yarn, approximately 10 inches from the ends. Repeat for the other side.

Silly Clown *(below, opposite)*

what you'll need

Red plastic funnel about 8 inches in diameter
Round white stickers
6 green chenille stems in varying widths
Hot-glue gun and hot-glue sticks
Tracing paper; pencil; scissors
Felt scraps in bright colors
Bright colored pom-poms
20-inch length of 1-inch-wide polka-dot ribbon
20 white paper coffee filters
Wide red marker; paper punch; cord

now make it together

1 If you can't find a red funnel, use red spray paint to cover the outside surface. Let dry. Apply round white stickers randomly to the outside surface.

2 Cut the chenille stems into lengths varying from 6 to 12 inches long. Group the chenille stems together, winding at the base. Hot-glue the group of chenille stems to the inside of the narrow end of the funnel.

3 Trace the flower and leaf patterns, *page 61*, onto a piece of tracing paper. Cut out and trace onto felt. Cut small colored flowers from felt. Snip a tiny hole in the center, insert chenille stem, and attach flower onto chenille stem with hot glue. Glue on center pom-pom. Tie leaf around green stem.

4 Glue a ribbon on each side of inside of funnel for ties.

5 To make collar, stack 18 to 20 coffee filters. While stacked, color around the edge of filters with a wide red marker.

6 Separate each filter, gently fold in half, and punch hole with paper punch in center, about ½ inch from fold. You will have two holes in middle of the coffee filter.

7 While still gently folded, string all coffee filters onto cord and tie around neck.

Grandpa Gus

what you'll need

Tracing paper
Pencil
Scissors
Long gray fake fur
Comb
Extra strong hair gel
Fine thread
Double-sided tape

now make it together

1 Enlarge and trace the patterns, *page 60*. Cut out and trace onto the back side of fake fur. We used long gray fur for our grandpa disguise.

2 Comb fur away from the pattern lines. Cut out the pieces.

3 Work enough hair gel into each piece to soak it. Shape each piece with fingers. Twist the ends of eyebrows and mustache into a narrow point. Comb the hair into the desired shape.

4 Use a piece of fine thread to tie tightly in the center of the mustache to give shape. Cut off extra thread. On gray beard, turn in edges and hot-glue to back.

5 Use double-sided tape to attach the hair pieces to your face.

(continued on page 60)

Talk With Your Kids

Talk about the different types of hats people wear and what headgear is worn in certain professions.

Family Disguises *continued*

....

Bright Idea
....
Make a variety of crowns to wear and pretend you are royalty.

Miss America *(page 59)*

what you'll need

Tracing paper
Pencil
Scissors
Crafting foam
White headband
Hot-glue gun and hot-glue sticks
White glue
Silver glitter
Gems
Beads or sequins on a string
White paper
Spray adhesive
2½-inch-wide gold ribbon

now make it together

1 For crown, trace pattern, *opposite*, onto tracing paper. Cut out pattern. Trace around pattern onto foam and cut out.

2 Center the foam piece on the headband and glue in place using hot glue. Let dry.

3 Coat the entire front of the foam piece with a generous amount of white glue. While wet, sprinkle glitter onto glue. Shake off excess and let dry. Add gems and trim as desired with hot glue.

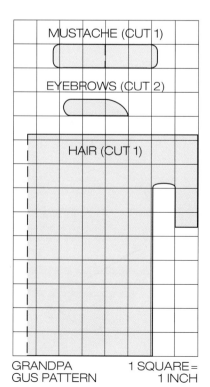

MUSTACHE (CUT 1)

EYEBROWS (CUT 2)

HAIR (CUT 1)

GRANDPA GUS PATTERN   1 SQUARE = 1 INCH

4 For banner, cut a piece of ribbon to fit around shoulder and down to the opposite hip. Type out the words "Miss America" on a computer and print on white paper. Cut words out as a strip. Cut additional strips of plain white paper to fit along entire ribbon. Spray adhesive onto the back side of the trimmed white paper strips. Let dry till tacky. Affix paper to ribbon. Glue ribbon ends together with hot glue to make a loop.

Grandma Gracie

what you'll need

Plastic headband
Gray yarn
Scissors; thick white crafts glue
Curlers
Bandanna or scarf
Cold cream, if desired
Tracing paper
Pencil
Purple crafting foam
Gems; ruler

now make it together

1 Cut groups of yarn from 10 to 36 inches in length. Keeping same lengths together, work with four strands at a time. Fold the group of strands in half. Place the loop under the headband. Thread the yarn ends through the loop and pull tight. Continue adding yarn to the headband until completely covered. Dab glue under the yarn at both ends to hold in place.

2 Cut three 12-inch lengths of yarn. Attach to center of headband in the same manner, except have tails ending on the other side of the headband for bangs.

3 Wrap the equal lengths of yarn in curlers. Continue until all yarn is in a curler.

4 To wear, place headband on, adjusting the curlers if necessary to cover head. Fold a bandanna in half with points together. Fold point toward center. Tie around neck.

5 For glasses, trace pattern, *page 61*. Cut out from purple crafting foam. Cut two ¼-inch slits in glasses front as shown on pattern. Glue gems as desired across top of frame. Let dry. Push ends of glasses bows through slits in the frame front.

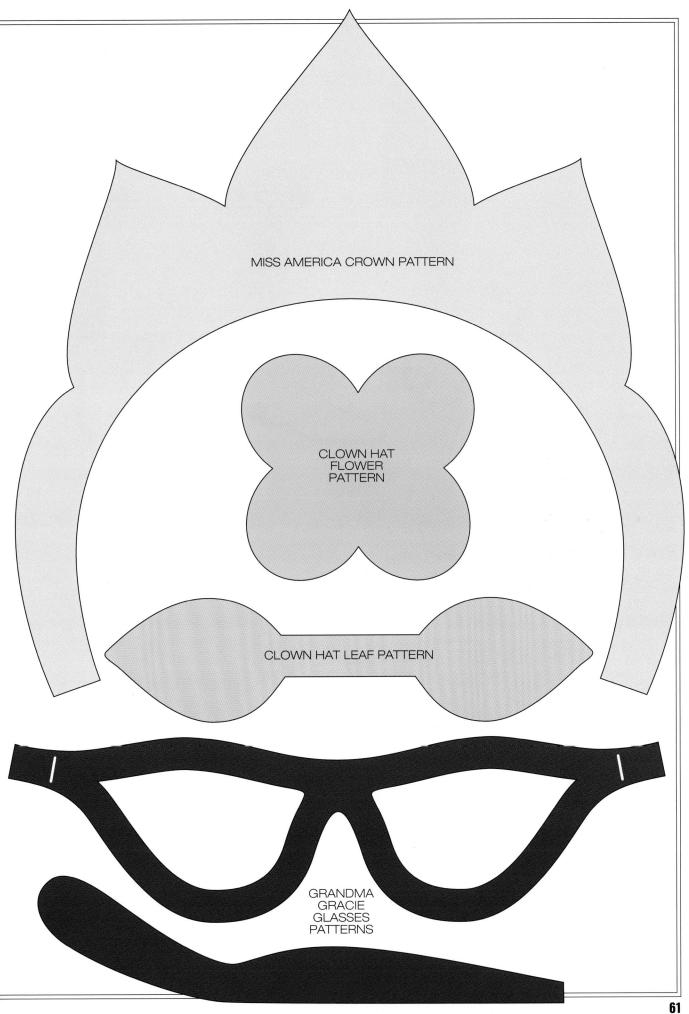

MISS AMERICA CROWN PATTERN

CLOWN HAT
FLOWER
PATTERN

CLOWN HAT LEAF PATTERN

GRANDMA
GRACIE
GLASSES
PATTERNS

Bright Idea
• • • •
To take these lights along when trick-or-treating, wrap the handles with reflective tape for safety.

Party Lights

Brighten your trick-or-treating with these cheery Halloween lights.

what you'll need
Translucent plastic tumblers
Flashlight
Clear packing tape
Permanent or paint marker

now make it together

1 Place the plastic tumbler upside down on top of the flashlight. Tape the tumbler to the flashlight with clear packing tape.

2 Using the photo, *above*, for inspiration, draw a face on the tumbler with a permanent marker or paint marker. Let it dry.

Glitter 'n' Bones

Here's an easy-to-make skeleton that will make almost anyone snicker.

what you'll need

White paper; scissors
Marker
Cotton swabs
Dark paper or cardboard
White glue
Glitter glue

now make it together

1 Draw a skull on white paper. Cut it out and glue it at the top of the dark paper.

2 Glue four swabs as rib bones below the skull. Then glue the spine on top of the ribs, making one end connect to the skull. Add arms extending from the top rib bone and legs from the bottom rib. Cut swabs into short pieces for fingers.

3 To give your skeleton pizzazz, dab glitter glue to its joints and facial features.

The Unscarecrow

This friendly fellow, which uses a body outline for the shape, greets visitors all autumn long.

what you'll need

2 sheets of foam-core board
Tape; pencil; crafts knife
Old clothing; burlap
Paints and brushes or marking pens
Straw hat
Scissors; removable poster putty

now make it together

1 Tape two sheets of foam-core board together. Place it on the floor. Lay down on the boards. Ask someone to help trace around your body shape. Carefully cut out.

2 Using old clothing, dress your scarecrow. Use burlap for the head. Use paints or markers to create eyes, mouth, and nose. Top with straw hat cut in half.

3 Use removable poster putty to hang the scarecrow on the door or wall.

Bright Idea
• • • •
Play a Halloween audio tape in your haunted house to add more excitement to the experience.

The Hall of Hands

A memorable addition to your next haunted house, this rib-tickling wall will bring both shrieks and giggles.

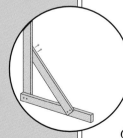

what you'll need
Large pieces of cardboard (available from appliance dealers, mailing service centers, or cardboard suppliers)
1×2 lumber; wood screws
Concrete blocks or sandbags
Colorful rubber gloves
Cotton or paper; crafts knife
Balsa wood slats
Feather dusters
Bubble wrap

now make it together
1 Make wood braces for two cardboard walls by screwing together 1×2s as shown, *left*. Position the walls close together to form a narrow hallway. Place concrete blocks or sand bags on the braces for support.

2 Stuff gloves with cotton or paper and balsa-wood slats. Cut small slots in the walls. Stick the slats and dusters into the slots.

3 Stick your hands into one pair of gloves to tickle guests. Put bubble wrap on the floor for fun popping noises.

Wart-the-Witch's-Nose Game

Entertain the crowd at your next Halloween party with this silly game.

what you'll need

Tracing paper
Pencil
Scissors
Large sheets of crafting foam in black,
  orange, and light lime green
Small sheets of crafting foam in purple,
  dark lime green, yellow, and white
16×20-inch piece of self-stick
  mounting board
Thick white crafts glue
1-inch tan felt furniture pads
Black thread
Needle
Double-sided tape

now make it together

1. Enlarge and trace the patterns, *pages 66–67*. Trace around the patterns on the corresponding colors of crafting foam and cut out.

2. Cut five stripes each from orange and black, each 2×16 inches. Remove the top sheet from mounting board, revealing the sticky side. Apply the orange and black stripes, alternating colors. Be sure not to stretch the pieces as they are applied.

3. Glue the hat to the top of the face. Glue the hair and shirt collar behind the head. Weave the hatband through the buckle. Glue to hat. Glue the stars and facial features in place. Glue to striped board. Let dry.

4. Thread the needle with a double strand of thread. Stitch through felt pads. DO NOT remove backing from pads. Use double-sided tape so the game can be used again and again.

5. To play, blindfold the player as he or she tries to place the wart on the witch's nose.

(patterns on page 66)

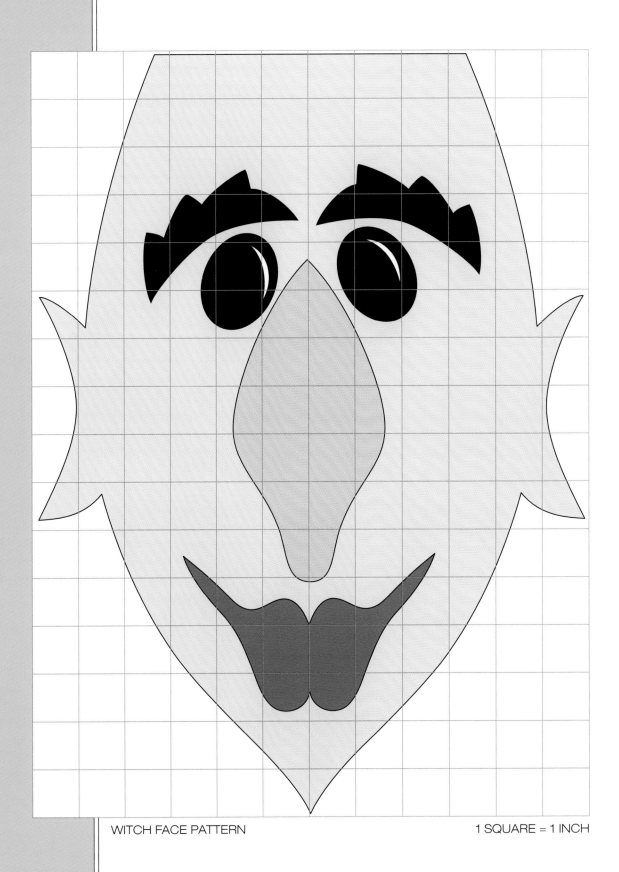

WITCH FACE PATTERN

1 SQUARE = 1 INCH

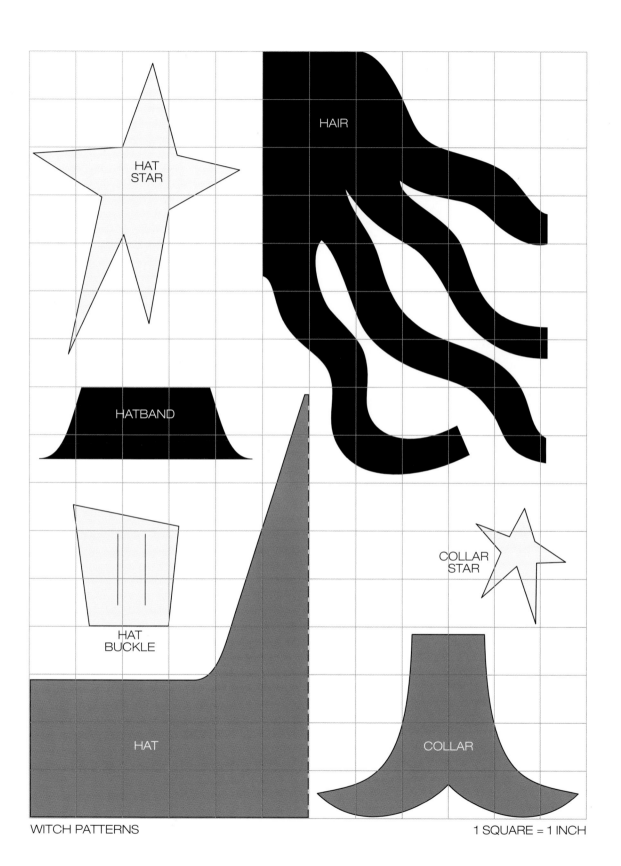

HAT STAR

HAIR

HATBAND

HAT BUCKLE

HAT

COLLAR STAR

COLLAR

WITCH PATTERNS

1 SQUARE = 1 INCH

Turkey Day Fun

When your family gathers on Thanksgiving Day, this turkey centerpiece will celebrate what each person is thankful for.

what you'll need

2 cardboard tubes, one approximately
  6 inches long and one about 1½ inches long
2 compressed-paper bowls
Acrylic paint
Paintbrush
Thick white crafts glue; clothespins
Construction paper
1 small round balloon
Toothpicks
Crepe paper in yellow and orange
Scissors

now make it together

1 Paint the longer tube and the undersides of the two bowls in desired colors. Let dry. Glue the rims of the bowls together so the undersides show. If necessary, clamp them with clothespins while the glue dries.

2 Glue the long tube along its length to one of the bowls. After the glue has dried, decorate the turkey by gluing crepe paper around the edges of the front bowl.

3 Cut out a construction-paper beak and eyes, and glue them to the top of the tube along with the balloon for the wattle. To make the turkey's feet, trace a child's hand onto construction paper; then cut it out and glue it to the bottom of the tube.

4 To make a pilgrim's hat for the turkey, cover the short tube with construction paper. Cut out a small circle top and a larger circle for the hat brim. Glue the hat pieces together; then glue the hat to the top of the longer tube.

5 Cut paper feathers from construction paper and glue toothpicks to their ends. Poke holes in the rear bowl to hold the feathers when they're brought to the table.

6 To add thankful sentiments, give each dinner guest a paper feather. Ask them to write or draw something for which they're thankful. Add the feathers to the centerpiece.

Talk With Your Kids
• • • •
Explain the importance of using good manners. Practice please and thank you. Discuss other ways to use manners.

Good Manners Napkins

These sweet napkins remind us to use good manners at the table.

what you'll need
Purchased cloth napkins; large pieces of paper
Pencil; fabric markers; scissors

now make it together
1 Decide what phrase to write (such as "chew with your mouth closed," "use your napkin," or "use your manners") on the napkin. Cut a strip of paper the length of the napkin. Use a pencil to write the phrase on the paper, adjusting to fit if necessary.

2 Use the paper strip as a guide to write the phrase on each edge of the napkin using fabric markers. Print with neat strokes. At the end of each line in a letter, add a dot in a contrasting color.

Wild Turkey

Take a walk in the wild to look for nature items to make this Thanksgiving pal.

Bright Idea
....
To make the paper turkey last longer, spray it with a coat of clear sealer.

what you'll need
Items from nature, such as pinecones, leaves, sticks, pebbles, bark, and seeds or kitchen items, such as bay leaves and dry bean soup mix
Colored poster board
Scissors
Pencil
Small plate
Thick white crafts glue

now make it together

1 First gather items from the outdoors, such as those listed at *left*.

2 Cut poster board to the desired size. On poster board, trace around a small plate for the body shape.

3 Starting at the outside of the circle, glue on small pieces in rows. Create a tail and feet from long pieces of nature items. Use bark for the head. Add eyes, a beak, and a red wattle. Let the glue dry.

Pilgrim Cap Place Cards

Welcome your Thanksgiving guests with these delightful personalized place cards.

what you'll need

3-inch terra-cotta flowerpot
Crafting foam in black, yellow, green, and purple
Scissors
Acrylic paints in black, white, red, green, and blue
Thick white crafts glue; black fabric paint pen

now make it together

1 Paint the entire pot black and allow it to dry. Choose a color to paint the band around the top of the pot. Let it dry. Make white dots on the rest of the pot by dipping the handle of a paintbrush in white paint and dotting onto the surface.

2 Cut a circle from black foam. Cut it about ½ inch wider all around than the pot opening. Use an appropriate size dish, cup, or lid to trace. Place a small amount of glue on the rim of the pot and glue onto the black foam circle.

3 To make the buckle, measure the width of the band of the pot (the portion painted a different color). Cut a rectangle out of foam that measures about ⅛ inch deeper than the band on the pot. Glue it to the band. Let the glue dry.

4 Use a black paint pen to write the guest's name on the colored band. Allow it to dry before using.

winter

Let the cold and snowflakes dance outside and find a warm cozy spot indoors for crafting. It's so much fun to spend family time together during this wondrous season of giving, creating heartfelt gifts and exchanging kind thoughts, merry wishes, and grand ideas. This chapter offers projects that use several techniques—from printmaking to sewing to painting. Treasure each moment you share together during the magical winter season.

crafting in winter

Count your blessings, including the gift of family and friends, during this heavenly season. There's no better time to handcraft cherished surprises for those you love and to get together to make decorations that make the season bright. Here we share dozens of ideas for the holidays as well as every day of winter. You'll be inspired to create merry memories that will last forever.

- Before the snow falls, go on a pinecone hunt. These nature items work wonderfully in winter wreaths, floral arrangements, and woodsy baskets.

- Plan a night to see the holiday lights around town. Invite an elderly friend to join you and share in the fun.

- Visit a local tree farm to learn about the varieties of Christmas trees. Purchase trimmings to make holiday wreaths and swags.

- Enjoy holiday music by going caroling, attending a concert, or listening to a new CD. Photocopy vintage holiday sheet music, trim it with decorative-edge scissors, roll it into scrolls, and tie it with a bow. Tuck the music scrolls in the Christmas tree for a musical tribute.

- Invite the neighborhood kids over to make holiday gifts and cards for their parents. You supply the crafting items; they'll supply the fun and laughter.

- Gather together as a family to make holiday greeting cards. When done in an assembly line fashion, you'll have plenty of cards for family and friends.

- Remember the birds during the cold months. Build a new bird feeder with each child in the family and let him or her keep the feeder filled throughout winter.

- Brighten the holidays (and the walkways) with handmade luminarias. Get the neighborhood involved and your whole street will glow with the magic of the season.

- Make heartfelt gifts for family and friends. Begin soon after Thanksgiving to avoid the last-minute rush.

- Clean out closets, toy boxes, and crafting supplies. Donate unwanted items to your favorite charity.

- Start a tradition of making a new ornament for the tree each year. Each family member can make one, making them alike or as different as desired.

- Go on a family outing to the library. Pick up a book about holiday customs throughout the world.

- Find construction paper, scissors, a paper punch, and yarn to make a valentine garland. Have each family member cut a variety of heart shapes from the paper. Punch holes on each side to thread yarn. If desired, trim the hearts with ribbon scraps, buttons, glitter, gems, and other items.

- If you're lucky enough to have snow, make a snow family that dances on your lawn. Instead of rocks, use big buttons for eyes and mouths. To color your characters, fill a spray bottle with water. Add food coloring and shake. Mist the merry snowpeople.

- Set aside a day for holiday baking. Let the kids help measure, pour, and mix. When everything is baked, pull up a step stool and let the kids wash the dishes. They'll have fun, and you'll appreciate the help.

- Give holiday goodies on festive plates. Use a paper punch to make holes around the edge of paper plates. Lace with pretty holiday ribbons and tie the ribbon ends into a bow.

- Have the kids draw winter and holiday scenes on paper. Trim and arrange on paper, leaving plenty of white space. Write a holiday letter in the white space. Take to a copy center to make copies and put them in the mail.

Lasting Impressions

Capture the symbols of the season with these fun-to-print cards!

what you'll need

Clean foam food tray, such as Styrofoam
Dull pencil
Washable paint
Paintbrush
Heavyweight paper

now make it together

1 Using a dull pencil, draw a picture in the bottom of a clean foam tray as shown in Photo A, *below.*

2 Brush washable paint over the drawing in the tray as shown in Photo B.

3 Lay a piece of paper over the painted area. Gently press down. Peel up the paper as shown in Photo C and let it dry.

A

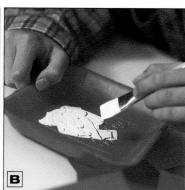

B

C

Pop-Up Fun

A simple pop-up technique makes for an impressive thank-you card.

what you'll need
Card stock
Scissors; glue stick
*Decorative motifs from kids' art,
recycled greeting cards,
postcards or other designs on
medium-weight paper*

now make it together

1 Fold a piece of card stock in half. Make two snips about 1 inch in length and 1 inch apart as shown, *below*.

2 Fold up the cut tab and crease it to create a step.

3 Cut out a design you like from a recycled card or kids' art. Paste the design to the rising part of the step. To hide the cuts, glue this card inside another piece of card stock cut to the same size.

POP-UP CARD
FOLDING
DIAGRAMS

Talk With Your Kids
• • • •
Remind kids of the importance of good manners. Helping them make and write their own thank-you cards is a good start.

Bright Idea
••••
Make small versions of these cards for holiday gift tags.

Merry Greeting Cards

These clever cards use fun techniques that will inspire card creation all year long.

what you'll need

Dark red matte card stock; paper plate
Acrylic paints in bright orange, deep red, and black
Plastic canvas
Sponge paint roller
Gold paper; scissors; decorative-edge scissors
Bright gold paint pen; glue stick

now make it together

1 Experiment with different colors of paper and paint. Our paper is a deep red and our paints are bright orange (much brighter than the paper), deep red (much darker than the paper), and black.

2 Spread paint onto plate in three separate areas. Use a sponge roller to apply paint. Soak it with water first. Squeeze out the excess water.

3 Lay a piece of plastic canvas over paper to be painted. Roll the dampened roller into paint, picking up some of all colors but very little of black as shown in Photo A, *below.* Paint in random strokes over the plastic canvas. Use a generous amount of paint and paint over areas if needed. Lift the plastic canvas occasionally to check the coverage as shown in Photo B. Let it dry.

4 Cut painted paper into desired shapes. Cut out shapes such as the star in the photo *above.* You can glue onto coordinating paper to create a border and show-through cutout. Use decorative scissors to cut edges if desired.

5 Use a gold paint pen to add designs or words to the card as shown in Photo C.

A

B

C

Fingerprint Gift Tags

Roll up your sleeves and get ready for some finger-painting fun!

what you'll need

Assorted paper
Decorative-edge scissors, optional
Colored ink pads; glitter glue

now make it together

1 Cut out or tear small pieces of paper to use as gift tags. If desired, trim the edges with decorative-edge scissors.

2 Press a fingertip on colored ink pad and then on the tags as shown in Photo A, *right*. Make holiday designs, such as wreaths, snowmen, and trees as shown in Photo B. Let the paint dry.

3 To add sparkle, if desired, apply glitter glue over areas of the design in the same manner.

A

B

Evergreen Greetings

Send holiday greetings in these quick-to-cut cards the whole family will enjoy making.

Bright Idea
. . . .
Use wrapping paper scraps instead of colored paper to make your holiday shapes for your cards.

what you'll need

Colored papers in blue, red, yellow, green,
purple, white, or other desired colors
Ruler
Pencil
Scissors
Tracing paper
Large paper punch
Glue stick

now make it together

1 Measure and cut the background paper to be 5×10 inches. Fold with the short ends together. Cut the next border piece to measure 4$\frac{1}{4}$×4$\frac{1}{4}$ inches. Glue in center of card front. Cut the tree background piece to measure 4×4 inches. Glue to the center of the card. Cut a white strip 3$\frac{7}{8}$×1 inch. Cut irregular scallops along one long edge for snow. Glue the strip at the bottom of the center square, leaving a hint of border color.

2 Trace the tree pattern, *left,* onto tracing paper and cut out. Trace around the pattern on green paper. Cut out. Glue the tree onto a piece of white paper. Trim the white paper close to tree, cutting a soft wavy line. Glue the tree in the center of the card.

3 Use a paper punch to make several circles from white paper. Glue the tiny white circles on the card to resemble snow.

TREE PATTERN

Talk With Your Kids
····
Remind your children of the true meaning behind the Christmas season and the kindness they can share.

Holiday Countdown Tree

As the anticipation of the season mounts, celebrate each day with this colorful tree that counts down the days to Christmas or the new year.

what you'll need

Felt in a variety of colors
Scissors
Pinking shears
Narrow ribbon
Thick white crafts glue
Large can
Colored paper, yarn, paint, or
  other desired trims
Stick
Rocks

now make it together

1 From felt, cut out 1½-inch-high numbers 1 to 25, adding 26 to 31 if counting down to the new year.

2 Cut a pair of 3×4-inch pieces from contrasting pieces of felt. Cut the long and one short end using pinking shears. Glue the pairs together, along the edges only of one short end and both long sides. Glue an 8-inch piece of ribbon inside open end. Let dry. Tie the ends into a bow. Repeat 24 or 30 times.

3 Glue the numbers onto one side of the felt rectangle. Let the glue dry.

4 Decorate the can using paper, yarn, paint, or other desired supplies. Place the stick in the center of the can. Fill the can with rocks. Fill the pockets with treats. Starting on December 1, hang the highest number on the tree. Each day hang another number on the tree, using consecutive numbers, for a sweet holiday countdown.

Artful Evergreen Ornament

In a few minutes, create trim-the-tree treasures for everyone you love.

what you'll need

Glass ornament
Low-temperature glue gun and glue sticks
Sheet of gold leaf (available at crafts and discount stores)
Soft cloth; paintbrush
Star sequins
Thick white crafts glue

now make it together

1 Use low-temp glue to make a free-form tree shape on the front of the ornament.

2 When the glue is dry, lay a sheet of gold leaf over the glue and rub gently with a cloth to adhere the gold leaf to the glue. Use a paintbrush to brush away excess gold leaf.

3 Use crafts glue to add star sequins to the treetop.

Bright Idea
• • • •
For a kid version of these ornaments, trim the top with tiny items such as dice, game pieces, play jewelry, or miniature toys.

Beribboned Ornament

For quick and easy ornaments, purchased trims are stunning Christmas ball toppers.

what you'll need

Ball ornament
Purchased satin ribbon flowers
Hot-glue gun and hot-glue sticks
1- to 1½-inch-wide ribbon in various lengths

now make it together

1 Decide how you want to make your ribbon topper. You can glue the satin ribbon flowers directly to the ornament top or to a ribbon bow you make.

2 Use hot glue to attach any ribbons and the ribbon flowers of choice. Let dry.

Talk With Your Kids
. . . .
Watch the movie *It's a Wonderful Life* together and talk about angels.

Dressed-in-White Angel

Make dozens of these heavenly trims with coffee filter gowns and wings.

what you'll need

3 coffee filters
3½-inch foam cone, such as Styrofoam
1 round toothpick
1-inch foam ball, such as Styrofoam
12 inches of ¼-inch-wide gold ribbon
White thread; hot-glue gun and hot-glue sticks
1 gold plastic ring

now make it together

1 Center one coffee filter on the top of the cone. Push the toothpick three quarters of the way into the cone and filter. Push the 1-inch ball onto the toothpick to add the head.

2 Center the second filter over the head. Tie a ribbon bow around the neck.

3 Fold the third filter in half and pleat at the center to form wings. Tie in the center with thread. Hot-glue the center of the wings to the back of the angel at the neck. Glue the ring to the top of the head for a halo.

Beaded Wreath Ornament

Add sparkle to a package or a special branch on the tree with these glistening, make-in-an-evening mini glass bead wreaths.

what you'll need

Spring bracelet wire
Wire cutters
Needle-nose pliers
Glass beads
⅛-inch-wide gold ribbon
Gold cord for hanging
Ruler

now make it together

1 Cut the spring wire into individual sections of 2½ coils each. Fold the end of the wire over with the needle-nose pliers.

2 Thread the entire length of wire with beads and then fold the end over with the pliers. Tie a ribbon bow on one side of the wreath bracelet and a hanging cord from the opposite side.

Beaded Bells

For bead-stringing lovers of any age, these ready-to-jingle bells are a joy to make.

what you'll need

Beading wire; wire cutters
Glass beads
2 jingle bells
Green ribbon
Cord or thin ribbon for hanging
Ruler

now make it together

1 Thread a 2-foot length of wire full of glass beads. Form the length of the beaded wire into a bell shape by bending it back and forth into approximately 14 rows. The first row should be about 1½ inches wide. The following rows should increase in width slowly until the last row is 3 inches.

2 Cut two lengths of wire, each 6 inches long. Thread the wire down through the end bead of each row. Use one wire for each side of the bell. These two wires will hold the bell together. Thread the jingle bells onto a 3-inch length of wire and twist them to the middle base of the bell.

3 Loop a hanging cord through the top of the bell and then tie a green ribbon bow to the hanging cord.

Shining Stars

These colorful ornaments sparkle with metallic paper, sequins, and jewels.

what you'll need

Satin ball ornaments in desired colors
Tracing paper; pencil; scissors
Metallic paper
Thick white crafts glue
Straight pins
Sequined or braided trim
Jewels
Sequins

now make it together

1 Trace the triangular pattern, *right*, onto a piece of tracing paper, cut out, and trace onto metallic paper of your choice. Cut 10 pieces for each ball you wish to make.

2 Glue triangles front to back with a straight pin sandwiched in between. The sharp end of the pin should extend at least ½ inch out the bottom of the triangle.

3 Begin pinning the triangles around the ball, forming a star shape. To fit, the triangles may need to overlap or have a small space between each piece, depending on the size of the ball ornament. Arrange the triangles so they are evenly spaced around the ball.

4 Use glue to add a trim around the ball where the triangles are attached, securing the triangles, trim, and ball together. Trim the outside of triangles. Embellish with jewels and sequins. Let the glue dry.

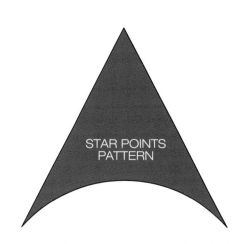

STAR POINTS
PATTERN

**Talk With
Your Kids**
····
Let stars be the topic of conversation. Talk about how they relate to Christmas, songs about stars, and favorite stars in the sky (or actors and actresses!).

Reindeer Face

Have a good time tracing your hands and shoes to make this member of Santa's herd.

what you'll need
Construction paper in red, white, black, brown, yellow, and green
Scissors; glue or tape; pencil

now make it together
1 For the head, trace around a large shoe on the brown paper. For the antlers, trace around your hands on yellow paper. Cut out the pieces.

2 Cut out two white circles and two smaller black circles for the eyes. Cut out a red circle for the nose. For the hat, cut out a red triangle, a white circle, and white "fur" trim. Cut out a green bow tie.

3 Glue the pieces together as shown in the photo, *above.*

Acorn Elves

Each of these little munchkins has a personality all its own.

what you'll need
Acorns with caps
Hot-glue gun and hot-glue sticks
Pistachio shells
Coriander seeds or similar size seed
Gold spray paint
Small paintbrush
Acrylic paints in red, green, and blue
Fine, black permanent marker
Drill with very fine bit
Fine gold wire
Wire cutters
Multicolored beads

now make it together
1 Wash and dry the acorns. Their caps may come off but can be easily glued back on.

2 Using a hot-glue gun, glue on ears and nose. Use pistachio shells for ears and coriander or similar seed for the nose. Glue the nose in the center of the face area, approximately one third of the way down, so it sits on the top portion of the face.

3 Lay acorns on paper and spray with gold paint. Let dry. Turn over and spray the other side. Spray a second coat if needed.

4 Paint caps any color desired with acrylic paint and a small paintbrush. Let dry.

5 Use a fine, black permanent marker to draw faces. Have fun making different expressions. The eyes are all drawn close to the nose and close to each other. To make round eyes, draw two small dots with a space between them. If desired, add eyelids as shown, *bottom left.* For sleeping eyes, draw short horizontal lines with the ends curved up slightly. Draw smile centered below the nose or place it off-center.

6 Drill small holes in stems with a very fine drill bit. String a 14-inch piece of very fine gold wire through hole. Bring ends up equally on both sides and twist wire together. String about 2 inches of multicolored beads onto wire.

7 Make a loop to hang ornament and string the loose end of wire back down into the beads until secured.

Moon Ornaments

Adorned with colorful nightcaps, these clay moons are easy to cut using a round cookie cutter.

what you'll need
Tracing paper
Round cookie cutter
Pencil
Paper
Scissors
Polymer clays in yellow, green, blue, purple, red, orange, and pink
Rolling pin
Decorative-edge scissors, optional
Needle
Glass baking dish
Gloss varnish
Paintbrush
Thread or fishing line

now make it together

1 Make a paper pattern using a piece of tracing paper and the round cookie cutter you intend to use for cutting dough. Trace a round circle from the cookie cutter. Slide the cookie cutter over to the right on your circle and draw another line to make a moon shape. Cut out the paper moon shape and use this as a guide for cutting uniform moon shapes.

2 Knead and roll out yellow polymer clay to about ⅛-inch thick. Using a circle cookie cutter, cut out round shapes. Lay down the paper moon guide onto the round yellow piece of clay and make a second cut with the cookie cutter.

3 Repeat the same process to make the hat. Roll out clay in color of your choice to ⅛-inch thick. Cut out a moon shape just like Step 2. Then make a third cut to turn the moon shape into a hat shape. Gently lay hat on top of yellow moon. Press and smooth into place.

4 Embellish hat with different colors of clay. Roll small balls and press onto hat to make polka dots. To make double-colored dots, stack dots on top of each other. Roll small strips of colored clay for stripes. Roll out thin pieces of clay and cut into shapes, using decorative-edge scissors if desired. Twist different colored strips of clay together to make trims. Roll a large pea-size piece of clay and press into tip of hat.

5 Using a needle, pierce a hole near the top of the hat large enough to insert thread for hanging.

6 Place on glass baking dish and bake in oven according to product instructions. Let cool before handling.

7 Brush on coat of gloss varnish. Let dry and tie thread or fishing line onto ornament for hanging.

Flocked Ornaments

Ornaments are the perfect item for decorating and giving—and these beauties will shine like the season itself.

Bright Idea
····
These trims can be fragile. To wrap as a gift, cushion the delicate ornaments by packing in fluffy garland.

what you'll need

Glass ornament, clear or colored
Flock in desired color (available as seasonal gift shops and crafts stores)
Thick white crafts glue
Ruler
Bottle cap
Paintbrush
⅛-inch-wide gold ribbon; scissors
Tinsel garland
Basket or decorative box

now make it together

1 For striped or polka-dot ornaments, squeeze dots or lines of glue around one half of the ball. Sprinkle flock over glue and gently press into glue. Rest ball, flocked side up, on top of a bottle cap. Let dry. Gently brush away excess flock. Repeat process for other half.

2 For ornaments with specific designs, thin glue with enough water to make glue brushable. Use a paintbrush to paint a design onto half of the ornament at a time. Sprinkle with flock and allow to dry. Brush off excess flock and repeat process for other half.

3 Cut a 12-inch length of ribbon for each ornament. Thread the ribbon through the ornament hanger, tying the ends into a bow. Trim the ribbon ends.

4 To display, hang the ornaments on the Christmas tree or place in a box or basket lined with tinsel garland.

Stacking Santas

As adorable as the stacking toys they resemble, this trio will bring ho-ho-hos to your holidays.

what you'll need

Dinner- and snack-size paper plates in
  holiday colors
Scissors; stapler; tracing paper; pencil
Thick white crafts glue
White felt; colored paper
Wiggly eyes, pom-poms, buttons or other
  desired trims
Embroidery floss in
  red or green

now make it together

1 Cut the paper plate in half. Overlap the cut ends and staple together.

2 Trace the patterns, *below*, onto tracing paper and cut out. Use patterns to cut face details and mittens from paper or felt.

3 Looking at the photo, *below*, for ideas, glue the pieces and trims in place. Let dry. Cut a 6-inch-long piece of embroidery floss. Knot ends. Push loop though hole at the top of each santa for a hanger.

Talk With Your Kids

····

Trace the history of wood stacking toys, beginning with their origins.

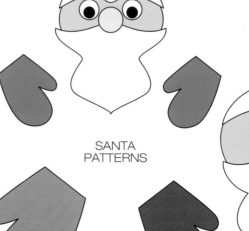

SANTA PATTERNS

Snip-Snip Ornaments

Snippets of embroidery floss splash color onto (or into) these clear holiday ornaments.

what you'll need
Bright colored embroidery floss; scissors
Small bowl
Glossy decoupage medium; paintbrush
Plastic or glass round ornament
Leather lacing in two colors
Thick white crafts glue

now make it together

FOR THE DECOUPAGED ORNAMENT

1 Remove the wrappers from embroidery floss. Cut the end loops with scissors. Cut each skein into tiny pieces, no larger than ¼ inch long. Put the pieces in a bowl.

2 Working in sections, paint the ornament with decoupage medium. Dip the ornament into the bowl of floss pieces until decoupage medium is covered. Continue adding decoupage medium and floss pieces until the entire ornament is covered. Let dry.

3 Paint a coat of decoupage medium over the entire ornament. Let it dry. Apply another coat if desired.

4 Cut a 12-inch length from the desired color of leather lacing. Curl and glue one end near the top of the ornament. Wrap the ornament top with the lacing, gluing to secure. Curl the remaining end and glue in place. Let the glue dry. Add a leather-lace hanger.

FOR THE FLOSS-FILLED ORNAMENT

1 Remove the hanger from the ornament. Gently fill the inside of the ornament with embroidery floss snippets in a mix of bright colors. Push into place using the handle of a paintbrush. Replace the hanger. Add a braided-floss hanger.

Bright Idea
····
Decoupage seed beads, confetti, or glitter onto your ornament.

Bouncy Bead Puppets

Adorable on a holiday tree or for the little ones to play with, these happy characters are made using a variety of beads.

what you'll need

Three 12-inch pieces of elasticized string
9 wood beads: 2 for the hands, 2 for the feet, 2 for the body, 1 for the head and 2 for the hat; miniature bell bead for the hat
2 buttons
Scissors
Permanent marker

now make it together

1 Cut three 12-inch-long pieces of string. Holding the strands of string together, tie them into a knot about 4 inches from one end. Cut off one long strand close to the knot.

2 Use the diagram, *below,* as a guide. For the feet, knot a bead onto the end of each of the two shorter strands.

3 For the body, pull remaining strands through the two body beads.

4 For the hands, knot a bead onto each of the two short strands.

5 Thread the remaining strand through the button, the head, another button, and then the hat beads. Tie the string end into a loop.

6 Using a permanent marker, draw a face on the bead that is between the buttons.

PUPPET
DIAGRAM

Santa's Helpers

Made from bits and pieces from around the house, these elves can become decorations or act as puppets for the next holiday play.

what you'll need

Cardboard tube
Acrylic paints
Paintbrush
Paper punch
Foam ball, such as Styrofoam, slightly larger in diameter than the tube
Straight pins
Felt scraps
Scissors
Construction paper
3 chenille stems
Pom-poms, buttons, markers, sequins, or other desired trim

now make it together

1 Paint the tube; let it dry. Punch two holes opposite each other at both the top and the bottom of the tube. With an adult's help, poke facial features into the foam ball with straight pins.

2 For the hat brim, cut peaks into a 6½×2–inch strip of felt or trace the pattern, *left*. Pin the brim in place around the head. Cover the top of the head with another piece of felt; push the edges behind the brim.

3 Make a paper collar by cutting a star shape slightly larger than the tube. Cut your own shape or trace the pattern provided. Poke a hole in the center.

4 For the arms, fold a chenille stem in half. Poke the folded end through the collar and into the base of the head. Bring the ends out through the holes on the tube top. Attach paper hands. For the legs, join the two remaining chenille stems. Thread them through the bottom holes. Fold the ends back for feet and attach paper shoes. Decorate the elf as desired using pom-poms, buttons, markers, sequins, and other trim.

ELF COLLAR

ELF HAT

1 SQUARE = 1 INCH

Talk With Your Kids
....
Share ideas for other types of paper garlands, such as those shown on this tree above.

Family Mitten Ornaments

Here's a great family activity that will result in this year's evergreen garland.

what you'll need
Construction paper
Crayons
Scissors; tape
Paper punch
Yarn

now make it together

1 Trace the hands of everyone in your family on brightly colored construction paper or card stock. To make a mitten shape, hold your thumb out and your fingers together. Cut them out and color them, adding personal touches.

2 Place a strip of tape along the top back of each mitten to reinforce the paper. Punch two holes through each mitten. String all the mittens together with yarn.

Peace Garland

Share joyful sentiments of the season with this graphic garland.

what you'll need
Marking pens in desired colors
White or colored index cards
Glitter glue
Mini stampers; ink pads
Paper punch; chenille stems

now make it together
1 Write a holiday message on white or colored index cards using marking pens. Write one letter on each card.
2 Decorate the cards with glitter glue and mini stampers.
3 Punch holes in the top corners. Link the cards together using chenille stems.

Bright Idea
····
To trim the cards or train, recycle other objects such as jar lids, buttons, and broken pieces of jewelry.

Train Garland

These paper choo-choos will delight all the little engineers.

what you'll need
Small cardboard tubes; ruler
Colored paper in red, green, blue, orange, and yellow
Glue stick; thick white crafts glue
Crafting foam scraps or plastic lids for wheels
Wooden stars; 2 craft sticks; scissors
Wooden spools or beads; 9-oz. plastic cups
Cord; darning needle

now make it together
1 Wrap each section of tube with a 4½-inch strip of colored paper. Secure with glue stick. Trace around the bottom of tube onto the foam to make circles for the wheels. Cut out the wheels and glue the tops to the sides of the paper-covered tubes. The wheels will hang down below the tubes. Glue two additional smaller wheels to each side of the train engine tube. Glue wooden stars to the center of all the wheels. Glue a craft stick across both sets of wheels on the engine.

2 Make two folds in a 4×2-inch rectangle of colored paper to make the engine cab. Cut a window in the two outer sections and then glue either side to the top of the engine car. Glue a spool funnel in front of the cab. Decorate the other cars with colored paper rectangles and stripes.

3 Cut the bottoms off the plastic cups. They will make the end caps to each train car. Carefully punch a hole in the center of the bottoms. Thread cord onto a darning needle and then string a cup bottom, paper tube, another cup bottom, and a spool. Repeat the process until all cars are strung. If you push the cup bottoms onto the train cars, they'll fit tightly.

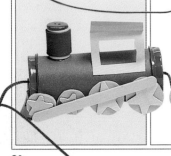

Jing-a-Ling Garland

Add holiday cheer with this playful bell garland made from a paper cup pattern!

what you'll need

Scissors; paper cups
Construction paper
Pencil
Assorted jingle bells (2 for each bell)
Metallic chenille stems
Decorative glue, such as confetti glue and
 glitter glue
Thick white crafts glue
Colored cord

now make it together

1 Make a pattern by cutting a slit down one side of a paper cup and removing the base. For each bell, lay cup pattern flat on paper and trace around it, adding a ¼-inch margin.

2 Decorate the paper with decorative glues as desired. Let it dry.

3 Cut out the paper shapes and glue them over the same size paper cups. Let the glue dry.

4 Poke the base of each cup twice with a pencil point. Fold chenille stems in half and thread the ends into the holes in each base, leaving a small loop sticking out.

5 Twist a jingle bell onto each end of the stem inside the bells. String the cord through the loops, knotting it at the top of each bell and spacing the bells several inches apart.

Talk With Your Kids

· · · ·

Talk about different bells—such as sleigh bells, steeple bells, and cowbells—and where you would hear them.

Bright Idea
· · · ·
Hang festive chenille stem garlands on banisters, mantels, and around doorways.

Chenille Stem Garland

These easy-to-shape garlands can be made short to trim the mantel or long to go around the entire Christmas tree.

what you'll need

Metallic chenille stems
Gold and pearl beads
Gold cord cut into 4-inch lengths
Scissors

now make it together

1 Thread gold and pearl beads onto the center of a metallic chenille stem. Spiral one end of the chenille stem up and the other end down. Repeat this process with all your chenille stems; then lay them out in a repeating color pattern.

2 Fold each length of cord in half and knot the ends together. Loop the cord into the spiral of one chenille stem and then connect it through the spiral of the next chenille stem. Use the knotted loops of cord to join all the spiraled chenille stems into a garland.

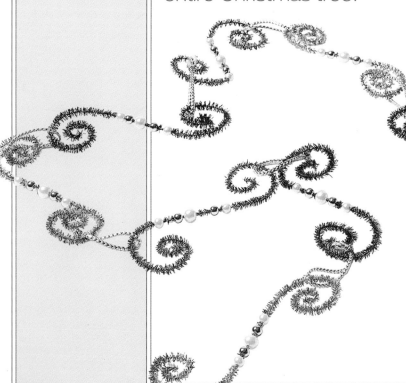

Whimsy Garlands

As much fun to string as they are to decorate with, colorful garlands add a playful touch to the tree.

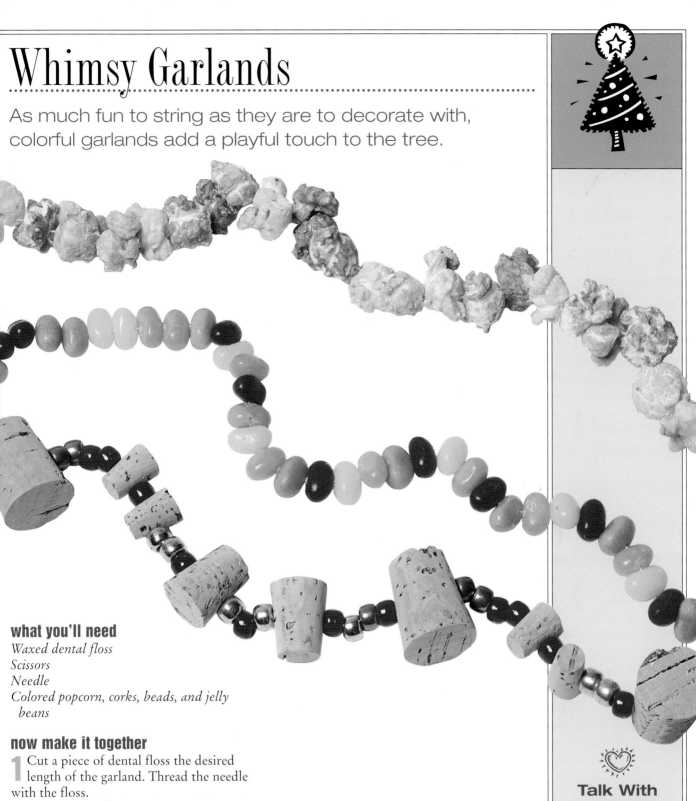

what you'll need

Waxed dental floss
Scissors
Needle
Colored popcorn, corks, beads, and jelly beans

now make it together

1 Cut a piece of dental floss the desired length of the garland. Thread the needle with the floss.

2 Push the needle through one object to be strung. Make a knot around the item to secure the end.

3 String on desired items randomly or in a pattern. Knot at the end.

Talk With Your Kids
····
Talk about the kinds of garlands you could make to feed the birds.

Fancy Boots

Just for giggles, trim old boots for one-of-a-kind holiday surprise holders for every member of the family.

what you'll need
Rubber boot
Spray adhesive
Assortment of fabric scraps
Scissors
Glitter fabric paint
Jewels, beads, sequins, or other desired trims
Sequined and braided trims
Hot-glue gun and hot-glue sticks

now make it together

1 Cut fabric pieces to fit the largest areas of the boot first, (for example, around the top portion). To fit fabrics around more difficult areas such as the ankles, it is easier to cut strips and fit into place. When your pieces are planned out and cut, you can apply spray adhesive to the entire outside of boot. Avoid spraying inside and on the bottom of the boot.

2 Apply fabric pieces to the boot until it is completely covered.

3 Cover uneven areas between fabric pieces by outlining the sections with glitter fabric paint. Let dry.

4 Embellish the boot sections with glitter fabric paint, beads, sequins, jewels, bows, etc.

5 Hot-glue trims to the top, bottom, and sections of the boot. Let dry.

Bright Idea
····
Use toddler boots to make individual party favors for kids.

Talk With
Your Kids
••••
Gather
together for
a history
lesson and
tell the kids
how the
tradition of
hanging a
stocking by
the fireplace
started.

St. Nick Stocking

Constructed from felt, this country-style Santa will dress·
up any mantel.

what you'll need

Tracing paper; pencil; ruler; scissors
½ yard of 45-inch-wide red felt
5x11-inch piece of hunter green felt
5x6-inch piece of ivory felt
3½x8-inch piece of cranberry red felt
2x2½-inch piece of tan felt
5x5-inch piece of cranberry red print fabric
5x5-inch piece of blue and black print fabric
Paperbacked iron-on adhesive; straight pins
Cotton embroidery floss: dark brown, ivory,
  blue, and red
Embroidery needle
Three ½-inch-diameter red buttons
Two ⅝-inch-diameter red buttons

now make it together

1 Trace one full stocking pattern and each individual piece from the pattern, *pages 100–101*, onto tracing paper. Cut two stockings from red felt. Cut heel and top border from green felt; scallop border and hearts from red felt; and the face, beard, mustache, and brim from ivory felt. Also cut a 1½x1-inch tassel strip from ivory felt.

2 Draw around circle, hat, and toe patterns onto paper side of iron-on adhesive. Reverse hat and toe patterns to allow for proper direction after fusing. Following

(continued on page 100)

manufacturer's instructions, fuse double-sided adhesive to backs of blue with black and red print fabrics. Cut out the pieces.

3 Remove paper backing from circle, hat, and toe pieces. Referring to stocking pattern, center circle 2½ inches below stocking top; fuse. Fuse toe piece over toe of stocking and hat in place atop circle.

4 Pin face, beard, and then hat trim in place. Using two plies of red embroidery floss and blanket stitches (see diagram, *opposite*) sew brim to stocking. Space the

stitches approximately ³⁄₁₆ inches apart. Use brown embroidery floss and blanket stitches to secure the outside edge of the beard and the edge to the left of the face. Make blue French-knot eyes. Use brown floss to work the eyelashes and to backstitch the nose. Attach the mustache with ivory floss running stitch through vertical center.

5 For tassel, cut ⅛-inch-wide fringe 1-inch deep across one long edge of tassel strip. Roll the strip and wrap with ivory floss ¼ inch down from the uncut rolled edge. Tack the tassel to the tip of the hat.

6 Pin the top border and scallop border in place, allowing scallop border to overlap bottom of top border. Using two strands of

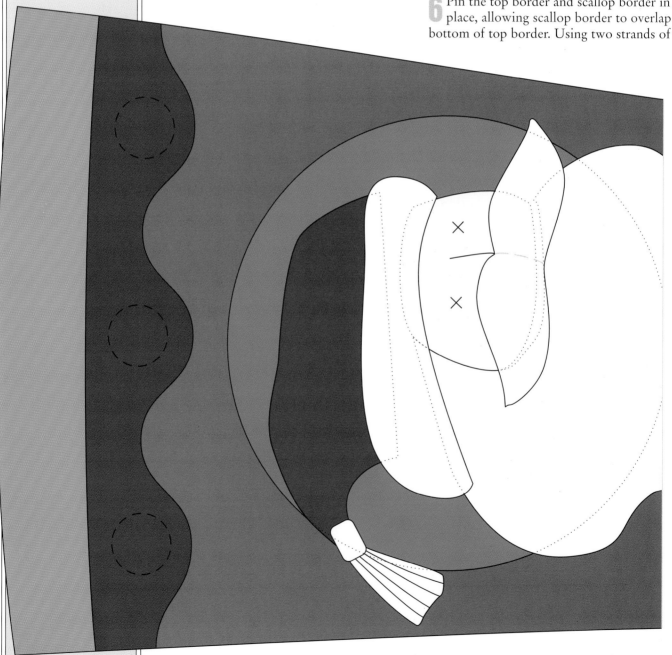

brown floss, sew along sides and tops of both borders using running stitches. Using red floss, sew one red button to each scallop.

7 Work large cross-stitches along the top edge of the toe piece using two plies of brown floss. Tack the hearts in place using red buttons sewn with red floss.

8 Cut two 12×¼-inch strips from green felt and one 12×¼-inch strip from red felt. Braid strips to make a hanging loop. Fold strip in half, stack ends, and tack to back side of stocking front at the outer top corner. Pin stocking front to back, wrong sides facing. Using the blanket stitch and two plies of red floss, sew the front to the back, securing the hanging loop.

BLANKET STITCH

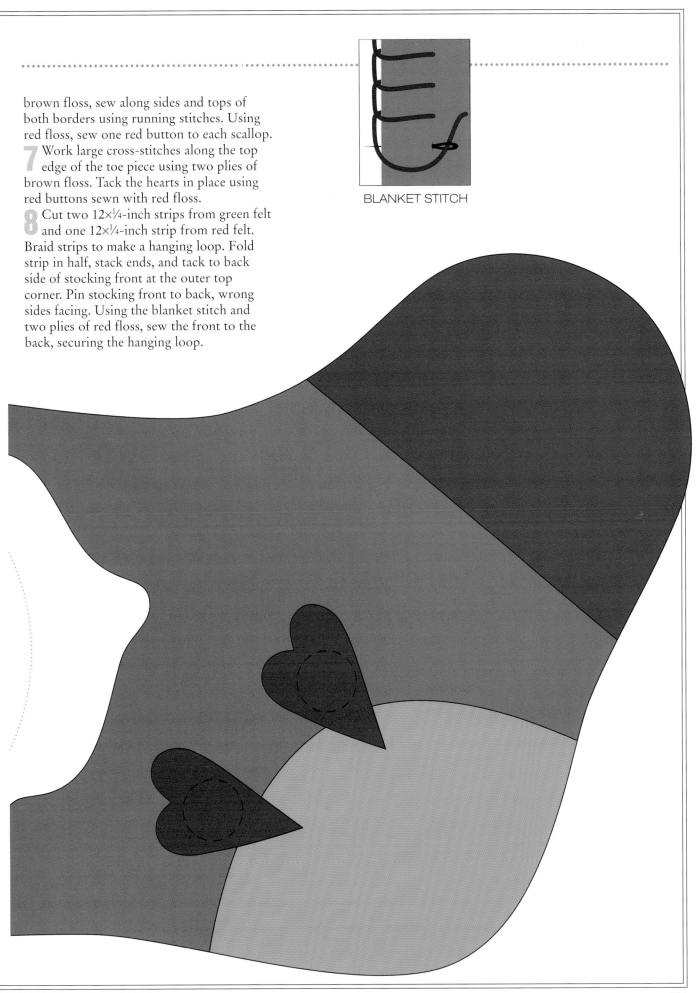

See-Through Decoration

Let the light shine through these tissue paper works of art.

what you'll need

*2 pieces of clear, self-adhesive vinyl, such as
  Con-Tact paper, cut the same size
Colored tissue paper
White paper
Tape*

now make it together

1 Create a holiday scene from pieces of tissue paper torn into various shapes. First lay out the pieces on a plain piece of paper or on a table. Transfer the scene, piece by piece, to a piece of the vinyl with the sticky side up.

2 Carefully add the second piece of vinyl to seal the picture. Tape the picture to a window.

Sparkling Cone Trees

Made from crepe paper, you won't have to worry about the needles dropping off these holiday trees.

what you'll need

Foam cones, such as Styrofoam
Crepe paper
Gold-head pins or straight pins
Gold star sequins
Gold beads
Thin chenille stems

now make it together

1 Starting at the base of the foam cone, wrap crepe paper around the cone working upward, overlapping the layers until the entire cone is covered. Insert a pin into the top of the cone to secure the crepe paper.

2 Decorate the tree by threading a gold bead then a star sequin onto a gold pin. Push it into the crepe covered cone. Repeat the process until the tree is completely decorated.

3 Thread three gold beads onto a chenille stem, fold the stem, and thread on three more beads. This creates one star point. Repeat the process to make five beaded star points. Twist the chenille stem ends together to form a star. Push the chenille stem end into the top of the cone.

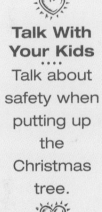

Talk With Your Kids
····
Talk about safety when putting up the Christmas tree.

Tumbled Candles

Candlelight is always wonderful, especially when the holder is crafted with love.

now make it together

1 Carefully cut holiday shapes out of the tissue paper.

2 Apply glue to the back of the tissue paper shapes and press them onto the outside of the tumbler. Experiment with layering colorful shapes over one another

Note: For safety, never leave a burning candle unattended.

what you'll need

Glass tumblers
Tissue paper in assorted colors
Glue stick
Small candle; scissors

Bright Idea
• • • •
Use these projects for clever organizers. Fill them with pencils, pens, rulers, paper clips, and more.

Plaid Painted Jars

Great for organizing dad's workshop, these painted jars are the perfect recycling project.

what you'll need

Clear glass jars with lids in a variety of sizes
Glass paints in desired colors
Paintbrush; permanent marking pens

now make it together

1 Wash and dry the jars and lids. Avoid touching the areas to be painted.

2 Paint vertical stripes on the jars using desired colors. Let the paint dry.

3 Paint horizontal stripes around the jars. Let the paint dry.

4 Paint the lids. Let dry. Use a marking pen to write content labels and to create designs on the tops of the lids.

Leather Lace Flowerpot

Give a fresh look to a terra-cotta flowerpot by adding stripes and swirls of colorful leather.

what you'll need
Ruler; leather lace in a variety of colors
Scissors; thick white crafts glue
Terra-cotta flowerpot

now make it together
1 Measure the rim of the flowerpot. Use this measurement to cut approximately 100 pieces from leather lace.

2 Glue lace pieces vertically around the rim of the flowerpot. When the entire rim is covered, cut two long pieces of lace to go around the top and bottom of the rim. Glue in place.

3 To decorate the bottom of the flowerpot, cut varying lengths of lace to make swirls, dots, and short lines. Glue in place. Let the glue dry.

Talk With Your Kids
Talk about colors and how to mix them together to make new ones.

Red+Yellow
=Orange
Yellow+Blue
=Green
Blue+Red
=Purple

Nifty Necklace

Using this fun technique, you can make a necklace to match any outfit.

what you'll need
Air-dry clay, such as Crayola Model Magic
Plastic lanyard long enough to fit around neck
Colored paper clips
Plastic straws in several colors
Washable paints; paintbrush; scissors

now make it together
1 Pinch small pieces of the clay as shown on the necklace, *right.* Poke a hole in each piece with a straw. Paint them and make patterns on the pieces with a straw or pencil. Let dry.

2 Cut some of the plastic straws into short pieces.

3 When the pieces are dry, line up the painted pieces, the straw pieces, and paper clips the way you want them arranged on the necklace.

4 String the pieces onto two pieces of lanyard. Tie a knot at each end. Tie together to form a necklace.

Bead Buddies

These charming characters make great best-pal gifts for boys and girls.

what you'll need

FOR REINDEER
2 yards of cord (plastic cord is easier to thread)
Beads: 68 light brown (body); 14 white (antlers); 10 cream (snout and belly); 6 dark brown (eyes and hooves); 1 red (nose)

FOR SNOWMAN
2 yards of cord (plastic cord is easier to thread)
Beads: 84 white (body); 18 brown (arms); 15 blue (hat); 2 black, 2 orange, 3 red (facial features); 3 green (buttons)

FOR RABBIT
2 pieces of cord, one 2 yards long and one 2 feet long (plastic cord is easier to thread)

Beads: 60 gray (body); 12 light purple (ears and belly); 2 black (eyes); 1 pink (nose); 3 cream (tail)
Knot the two cords together, and start in the middle. Pair the long cord with the short cord to make the ears. After threading the short cord through the nose, leave the ends as whiskers.

FOR BEAR
2 yards of cord (plastic cord is easier to thread)
Beads: 99 yellow (body); 2 brown (eyes); 1 tan (nose); 21 cream (snout and belly)

now make it together

1 Measure the amount of cord you'll need for the project you choose. Fold the cord exactly in half, and tie a small knot at the folded end.

2 String the beads for the first row onto the right cord, following the diagram. Then push the left cord through those beads, from left to right. String the second row of beads onto the right cord, and weave the left cord through them, left to right. Continue in this manner, stringing beads onto the right cord and weaving the left cord through them.

3 For arms, legs, tails, or ears, string all the beads you'll need in a single row on one cord. Line up the beads in rows on the cord to make the desired shape. Loop and weave the cord back through the rows to make the shape you want. Bring the part up to the body, tighten the cord, and tie a knot.

4 When you're done, tie a knot in the end and trim the cord.

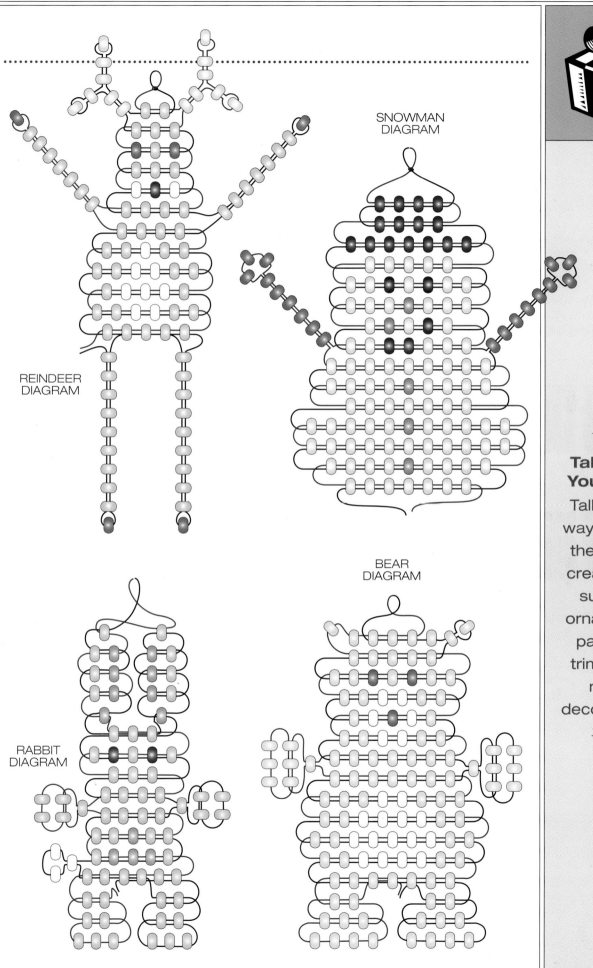

SNOWMAN
DIAGRAM

REINDEER
DIAGRAM

BEAR
DIAGRAM

RABBIT
DIAGRAM

**Talk With
Your Kids**
····
Talk about
ways to use
their bead
creations—
such as
ornaments,
package
trims, and
room
decorations.

Bright Idea
····
Frame things other than photos, such as good report cards, art, favorite sayings, and poetry.

Terrific Tile Frames

On your next trip to the home improvement store, pick up ceramic tiles to make these fun frames to give as gifts.

what you'll need

Scissors; photograph
Spray photograph adhesive
Colored mat board
Cotton ball; rubbing alcohol; tile
4 rubber, foam, or cork bumper pads
Decorative trims; decoupage medium
Damp cloth
Ceramic, glass, or tile paint; paintbrush
Easel or adhesive hanger

now make it together

1 Trim the photo as desired. Using spray adhesive, spray the back of the photo and center it on the mat board. Trim the mat board to allow a narrow border to show (see Photo A, *below*). Clean overspray with a cotton ball and rubbing alcohol.

2 Position the mounted photo squarely on the tile in the desired location. Use this as a guide for placing the bumpers. For the bottom two bumpers, clip a 90-degree corner out of each with scissors. For the top two bumpers, cut them in half and place each as shown in Photo B. This allows the photograph to be removed or replaced.

3 Remove the photo before decorating the tile. Decorate the frame and bumpers with decorative trims and covers as desired. When applying a thin braid, dip the entire piece in decoupage medium and position it as desired (see Photo C), cleaning off the excess with a damp cloth. Let dry. If painting the tile, bake it in the oven as instructed by the paint manufacturer. Place the photo in the frame and set it on an easel or attach an adhesive hanger to the back.

A

B

C

Clothespin Kids

There is no end to the friends you can make (or give)—all from little clothespins!

what you'll need

Small flat clothespins
Paint and fine paintbrush or ultra-fine marking pens; ruler; wood craft sticks
Cotton embroidery floss in desired colors
Thick white crafts glue; tape
3/8×1-inch wood craft ovals; white paint
Paintbrush; scissors

now make it together

1 Paint or draw a face on each clothespin head as shown in Photo A, *right*. We used black for the eyes, lashes, eyebrows, and nose. We used red for the mouth and pink for the cheeks. If desired, add a tiny dot of white to each eye for a highlight.

2 Cut a 7/8-inch-long piece off the rounded end of each craft stick for the arms.

3 Choose the floss color(s) for the sweater. Start by gluing the end(s) of the floss to the back of the clothespin, just below the head (Photo B). If using two colors, hold them together without twisting and wrap the clothespin to the waist, making stripes.

4 Wrap two arms to match sweater for each doll, leaving the rounded end of the craft stick showing for the hands. Glue the arms to the shoulders.

5 Beginning at the bottom of the sweater, wrap the floss for the pants down over the hips and down each leg, ending 1/2 inch above the end of the clothespin.

6 Wrap the floss for the boots from the bottom of each pant leg to the end of the clothespin.

7 For the girl's hair, cut fifteen 2-inch-long strands of floss. Lay the strands side by side and tie them together in the center as shown in Photo C. Glue the center to the top of the head. Gather half of the hair on each side of the girl's head and tie with a floss bow to make pigtails.

8 For the boy's hair, cut tiny snips of floss and glue them to the top of the head.

9 For the boy's hat, cut six 8-inch-long strands of floss and knot the strands together at one end. For braided hat, tape knot to the table. Braid the strands loosely, using two strands for each ply of the braid as shown in Photo D. When the braid measures 3 inches, knot the ends. Trim the floss to 1/4 inch beyond the last knot for the pom-pom. Wind and glue the braid around the top of the head starting with a circle and ending with the pom-pom on top.

10 For soldier's hat, cut a 1-inch section from the floss wrapper. Trim one end, leaving a short, rounded brim as shown, *left*. Add a small tassel to the front. Glue to the soldier's head.

11 To make doll stands, paint the wood ovals white. Let them dry. Glue an oval to the bottom of each doll.

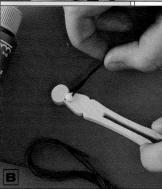

A

B

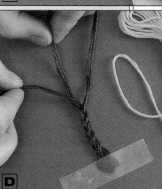

C

D

109

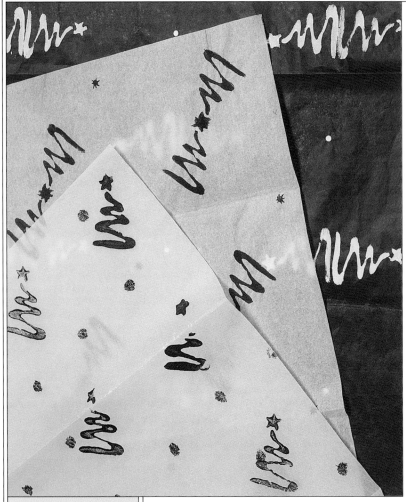

1 Draw a simple design on a 2-inch-square piece of paper. If desired, trace a stencil of your choice.

2 Lay the self-adhesive foam down with the paper back facing up. Place the transfer paper on the foam back and the design on top of the transfer paper. Trace the design. Carefully cut out the design using a crafts knife. After cutting out the design, cut out the surrounding 2-inch square. Trace the 2-inch square onto the foam board twice. Cut out these two squares.

3 On one foam board square, place the self-adhesive surrounding foam design. Trace the original design onto the second foam board piece and adhere the cutout designs in place.

4 Choose the color of paint and the color of tissue paper desired for the wrapping paper. Spread newspapers on the work surface and lay down your tissue paper. Pour a small amount of paint on a paper plate.

5 Paint the stamp with a paintbrush. Stamp the tissue paper in the corner, pressing firmly. Using a paintbrush rather than dipping the stamp directly into paint makes a sharper image. To prevent tears, hold the tissue paper down while gently pulling up the stamp. After each stamp, carefully pull the tissue paper up so that the paint does not dry to the newspapers below. Using the same stamp, apply paint again and repeat. This stamp will be placed diagonally from the top corner of the first one. The third one will be done diagonally from the previous lower corner. Repeat these steps until the entire paper has a checkerboard effect. For a different design, stamp randomly on the tissue paper.

Bright Idea
····
Experiment with the stamps. Change the placement of the stamp to create a new design.

Stamped Wrapping Paper

Personalized wrapping and tissue papers make gifts more special.

what you'll need
Paper; pencil or pen
Ruler
Christmas stencils, optional
Self-adhesive foam 2mm thick
Transfer paper; crafts knife
½-inch-thick lightweight foam board
Acrylic craft paint in desired colors
Paintbrushes
Paper plate
Tissue paper in assorted colors
Paper towels; newspapers

Reindeer Wrap

Gracefully leaping, these prancing reindeer turn ordinary craft paper into a glorious wrap for the holidays.

what you'll need

Tracing paper; pencil; scissors
Card stock
Newspaper
Brown craft paper
Spray adhesive
Tan spray paint
Red acrylic paint
Sponge cut into star shape

now make it together

1 Trace the reindeer pattern, *below*, onto tracing paper. Cut out the reindeer shape and trace around it on card stock. Cut out the center of the shape to create a stencil. Cut out eight to ten stencils.

2 Spray the back sides of the stencils with a light coat of adhesive. It should be tacky enough to hold in place but not stick firmly.

3 Place the stencils randomly onto the craft paper, overlapping the edges. If needed, fill in in any uncovered areas between the stencils with pieces of newspaper.

4 Lightly spray several coats of spray paint onto the craft paper to reveal the deer stencil. Let dry and remove stencils.

5 Add red stars between the deer using a sponge. Soak the star-shape sponge in water and squeeze out the excess. Dab the sponge in red paint, and randomly stamp onto the surface. To make red dots, dip the eraser end of a pencil into paint and dot onto the surface. Let the paint dry.

Talk With Your Kids

Talk about the symbols of the season, ones which are your favorites.

REINDEER PATTERN

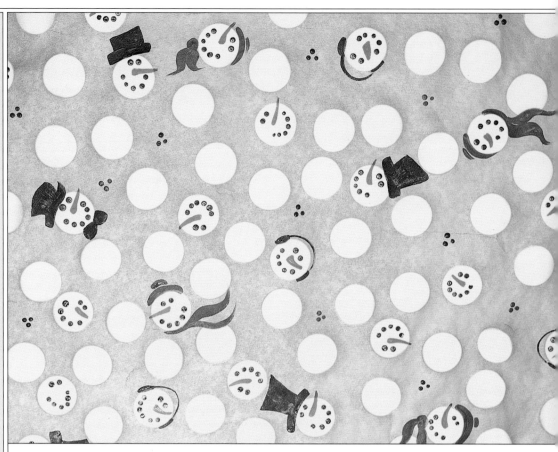

Bright Idea
••••
For other celebrations, use this same technique to make happy faces, animal faces, clowns, or other favorite images.

Rolling-Snowmen Wrap

A scattering of poker chips and a can of spray paint make the background for this festive paper.

what you'll need
White butcher paper
Poker chips
Gold spray paint
Acrylic enamel paints in desired colors
Paintbrush

now make it together

1 In a well-ventilated work area, lay out desired length of butcher paper. Weigh down the ends if the paper wants to roll.

2 Scatter poker chips on paper. Adjust if necessary so that no chips overlap. Spray the paper with gold spray paint. Let it dry. Remove the poker chips.

3 Use acrylic paints to add face details, hats, and scarves in varying directions. Let the paint dry.

4 To add small dots between large white dots, dip the handle of a paintbrush into paint and dot in groups of three on paper. Let the paint dry.

Fallen-Snowflake Paper

Have the kids cut out dozens of paper snowflakes to create this wintertime wrapping paper.

what you'll need

Printer paper
Scissors
Iron
White butcher paper
Spray paint in desired colors

now make it together

1 Cut snowflakes from printer paper. To make snowflakes, fold printer paper in half. Fold in half again along fold. Bring folds together one or two more times, creasing as you go. Cut notches and designs along outer edges and folds, being careful not to cut all the way across. Unfold the cut paper. Using a low setting, iron the snowflakes flat.

2 In a well-ventilated work area, roll out the desired length of white butcher paper. Weigh down the ends of the butcher paper, if needed, to avoid rolling. Lay the snowflakes on the paper, arranging until the desired look is achieved.

3 Carefully spray-paint over the snowflake cutouts, being sure to spray from directly above so the snowflakes do not shift. Use one color or overlap colors if desired. To make a large sheet, move snowflakes as necessary to complete area. Let the paint dry. Remove the snowflakes.

Talk With Your Kids
· · · ·
Talk about how snow is formed and what areas of the world do not get snow.

**Bright
Idea**
····
To make
several of
these
festive
bags, start
with brown
paper lunch
sacks.

Reindeer Bags

Untraditional color combinations give these reindeer a funky makeover.

what you'll need

Crayons
Paper gift bag
Construction paper
Tracing paper; pencil
Scissors
White glue
2 chenille stems
Large and small pom-poms

now make it together

1 With crayons, draw two legs on the wide sides of the gift bag. Than draw the fronts and backs of the legs on the other sides of the bag.

2 Trace the pattern, *opposite.* Cut out. Use the pattern to cut a construction paper head. Color in the details as desired.

3 Glue the head to the top front of the paper bag.

4 Bend the chenille stems into antler shapes and glue them between the bag and the paper head. Glue on a pom-pom nose and in the eye centers. Let the glue dry.

REINDEER BAG
PATTERN

**Talk With
Your Kids**
· · · ·
Talk about
reindeer—in
what parts
of the
country they
live, what
they eat,
and how
they differ
from other
deer.

115

Wood Menorah

Light up the season with these colorful candleholders.

what you'll need
Wood beads, wheels, and spools
Acrylic paints in desired colors
Paintbrush
Chenille stems
Thick white crafts glue
Fabric paint pens
Birthday candles
Plastic birthday cake candleholders
Small metal washers

now make it together
1 Paint wood pieces solid colors as desired. Let them dry.

2 To make candlestick, slip several painted wood pieces onto a doubled chenille stem that is covered with glue. Let dry. Decorate the candlesticks with paint pens, as desired. Slip a candle into a plastic candleholder and then slide the holder through a metal washer and into the hole of the top bead of the candlestick.

Noah's Ark Menorah

Bright colors combine to make this playful menorah a family favorite.

what you'll need

Oven-bake clay, such as Sculpey, in desired colors; plastic knife; toothpicks, optional
Small candles; acrylic paints; paintbrush
Permanent marking pens; pencil

now make it together

1 Using the photographs, *below*, for inspiration, form the clay into a Noah's Ark for the servant candle (the shammes). Create four pairs of animals, such as giraffes, snakes, alligators, and birds. Keep the bottoms flat so the pieces will stand up when done. Tips for making some of the pieces:
FOR THE ARK, start with a canoe-shape base. Add a small square on top. For the roof and ramp, you can roll the clay flat with a rolling pin or press down on the clay with your hands and cut out the shape with a plastic knife. Add a small door. To make impressions for texture, press a plastic knife into the clay.
FOR THE BIRD, form a pea-size piece of clay for the head. Roll a slightly larger ball for the body, forming into a teardrop. Add tiny clay wings. For eyes, make indentations using the point of a pencil.
FOR THE GIRAFFE, roll four 1-inch-long legs, an egg-shape body, a thick neck, head, ears, and antlers. Press parts together, adjusting legs so the piece will stand up. Make eyes with a pencil.
FOR THE SNAKE, roll a thick coil, shaping as desired. Add a tongue. Make eyes with a pencil.
FOR THE ALLIGATOR, form a long shape, slightly larger than a hot dog. Use a knife to make a cut in one end for the mouth. Push in small pieces of toothpicks for teeth. Make pinches along the top back. For eyes, roll two pea-size balls. Press pieces together.

2 Push a candle into the top of each clay shape. Remove the candles and bake the clay according to the manufacturer's instructions. Remove the clay shapes from the oven and let cool.

3 If desired, decorate the pieces with paint or marker. Let dry.

Talk With Your Kids
....
Talk about the meaning of the menorah and the traditions you celebrated as a child.

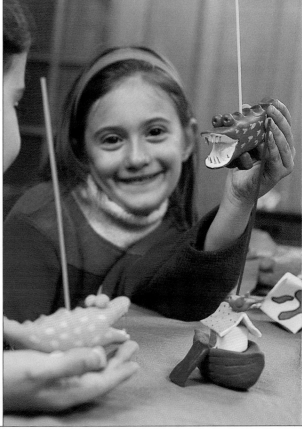

Star-of-David Party Favors

Ready for tiny toys, chocolate coins, and other treats, these mini containers add a festive touch to the party.

Bright Idea
. . . .
Send the kids on a scavenger hunt by giving them clues to where their party favors are hidden.

what you'll need
Dinner plate; colored paper; pencil
Scissors; tape or thick white crafts glue

now make it together

1 Trace around a dinner plate on colored paper and cut out the circle shape. Cut the circle in half.

2 Fold one of the half-circles in half three times, forming a fan of wedge shapes. Cut a point at the wide end through all the layers. Open up the shape and cut away one of the pointed wedges.

3 Tape or glue the fan into a cone shape, overlapping two wedges. Fold back the points to form a six-pointed star.

Pencil-and-Paper Dreidels

Perfect party favors, kids will love these spinning symbols.

what you'll need
Paper
Ruler
Scissors
Paper punch
Marking pens
Double-sided tape
Pencil; stapler

 A

 B

now make it together

1 Fold an 8½×8½-inch square of paper into quarters. Open up the shape. Paper-punch a hole in the center of the paper.

2 Referring to the diagrams, *above*, fold the corners of the square into the center (A). Flip the shape over and fold the corners into the center again (B). Flip the shape over. Draw the Hebrew letters Nun, Gimel, He, and Shin on the four squares.

3 Slip your fingers inside the four square pockets and bring the corners together. Wrap a piece of double-sided tape around the pencil about 2 inches from the sharpened end. Slip the pencil through the hole from the top of the paper shape, press the shape to the tape on the pencil, and then staple the underside folds together. Push the top four squares of the shape toward the pencil.

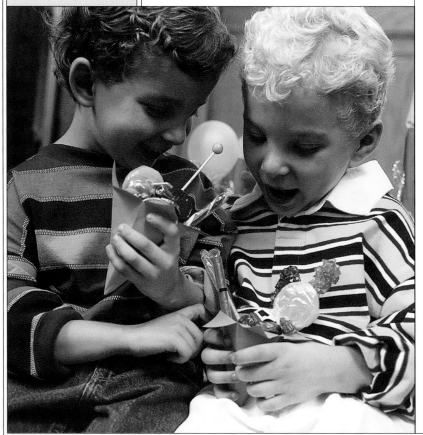

Drawstring-Bag Invitations

Start the party off with a bang, using these clever invitations to set the mood.

what you'll need

Large plate
Fabric scrap
Scissors
Thread
Needle
Yarn
Beads
Permanent marking pen
Chocolate coins

now make it together

1 Trace around a large plate on fabric. Cut out the circle.

2 Turn under a narrow hem around the outside edge, baste it, and thread a length of yarn through it. Tie a bead at each end of the yarn.

3 Turn the hemmed side over and write the invitation message with a marker or pen. Pull up the gathers, fill the bag with chocolate coins, and tie it shut.

Talk With Your Kids
····
Talk about ways to make guests feel welcome in your home.

Friendly Frosties

Imagine these welcoming snowmen lighting your Christmas walk.

now make it together

1 In a well-ventilated work area, spray-paint the fishbowls. Let dry.

2 To make a nose, form a carrot shape from orange clay. Push a golf tee in the wide end for extra strength. Place on baking dish. Bake in the oven according to the manufacturer's directions. Let cool.

3 Glue a clay nose on each fishbowl. Let dry. Use glass paint to make the eyes and mouth. Paint quarter-size dots for the eyes and smaller dots for the mouth. To make snowman winking, paint one eye as shown, *below*, with eyelashes in the corner.

4 To make a hat, wear work gloves. Cut an 18-inch circle from crafting mesh. Center the mesh over the can. Form the mesh over the can, folding the edge into a brim. Tie a ribbon around the brim.

5 Put a tea candle in the luminaria. Place the hat on top of the luminaria.

Note: For safety, never leave a burning candle unattended.

what you'll need
Round fishbowls
White frost spray paint
Orange oven-bake clay, such as Sculpey
Golf tees; glass baking dish
Black glass paint
Paintbrush
Silicone glue, such as E6000
Crafting mesh; work gloves
Old scissors; ruler
Round can, such as an oatmeal container
Ribbon; tea candle

Bright Idea
. . . .
Organize a luminaria-making party for the neighborhood so everyone can enjoy these smiling snow guys.

Talk With
Your Kids
....
Brainstorm
non-
flammable
items that
would work
in these
luminarias.

Canning Jar Luminarias

Even when guests are about to arrive, there's time to make a small collection of these pretty candles.

what you'll need

Canning jars without lids
Nonflammable items, such as buttons, unwrapped candies, marbles, or aquarium rocks
Votive candle cup
Votive candles
Ribbon, if desired; scissors

now make it together

1 Remove the lid from the canning jar. Wash the jar. Let it dry.

2 Fill the jar approximately halfway with desired filler, such as buttons, unwrapped candies, marbles, aquarium rocks, or other nonflammable items.

3 Place the candle in the votive cup. Nestle the cup in the center of the filler.

4 If desired, tie a ribbon around the neck of the jar. Trim the ribbon ends.

Note: For safety, never leave a burning candle unattended.

Sparkly Snowflakes

These three-dimensional, sparkly paper snowflakes are just like the icy cold variety—no two will ever be the same.

what you'll need

Lightweight printer paper
Scissors
Pencil
Lightweight string
Glue stick
White glitter

now make it together

1 Fold piece of printer paper in half, with the long edges together.

2 Unfold the paper and cut along the fold line.

3 Starting at the short end, fold the paper like a fan every ¾ inch, keeping the edges even as shown in Photo A, *below*.

4 Cut a small V notch in the center of each fold as shown in Photo B. The notch lets the snowflake open and glue easily. Tie a piece of string around the notch. Cut desired designs along outer edges and folds (Photo C), being careful not to cut all the way across.

5 Fold the paper ends together and glue as shown in Photo D. Trim the string or use it to hang the snowflake.

6 Glue glitter to the snowflake edges or on the front of the snowflake.

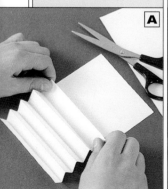
A

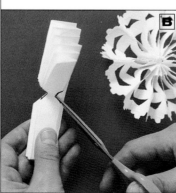
B

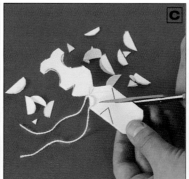
C

D

Dancing Snowmen Jars

There's no man like snowman, especially when he playfully watches over sweet treats.

what you'll need

Glass jars or candy jars
White air-dry clay, such as Crayola Model Magic clay
Metallic-colored crafting wire
Wire cutters
Ice pick
Metallic-colored beads
Clear adhesive, such as E6000
Acrylic enamel paints in black and white
Toothpicks
White glass paint
Pencil with round-tip eraser
Assorted ribbon

now make it together

1 Wash the jar. Let it dry. Avoid touching the areas to be decorated.

2 Shape two or three small balls from clay for each snowman. Press together. Lay jar on its side. Place snowman in position on jar and press gently against glass.

3 Cut and shape wire arms, nose, and hat, if desired. To make a small cone nose, wrap wire around the end of an ice pick. While the clay is still moist, push wire pieces in place. Turn slightly to secure. Push beads into place for buttons. Let clay dry on jars.

4 Remove clay shapes from jar and glue back in place. Let the glue dry.

5 Use a toothpick dipped in paint to add eyes and a mouth.

6 If desired, add polka dots to the candy jar lids. Dip the eraser end of a pencil into white glass paint and dot onto the surface. Let the paint dry.

7 Tie ribbon bows around the jar tops. Trim the ribbon ends.

Talk With Your Kids
. . . .
Retell the Frosty the Snowman story together, letting each family member tell a part.

Silly Snowballs

A silly decoration all winter long, these personality-plus snowballs can be grouped in a bowl or stuck to a window so they appear to be flying.

what you'll need

4-inch foam ball, such as Styrofoam
Table knife
Foam balls, such as Styrofoam, in various sizes
White air-dry clay, such as Crayola Model Magic clay
White glitter
Blue beads
Spoon
Pencil with round-tip eraser
Removable poster putty

now make it together

1 On a well-protected work surface, cut a 4-inch foam ball in half with a table knife. This will be used for the top snowball, *left*.

2 Roll out smooth pieces of white clay about ¼-inch thick and smooth around foam balls and a ball half as shown in Photo A, *below*. Make small round balls for eyes and noses (Photo B). Press in two small blue beads for the eyes. Make the eyebrows with small pieces of rolled clay. Make different shaped mouths with the eraser end of a pencil, as shown in Photo C, or use a spoon.

3 Sprinkle white glitter onto clay while it is still moist. Roll around on clean surface to press in glitter.

4 Let the pieces dry. To hang, use small amounts of removable poster putty to stick the balls together and stick to windows.

Snowman Snow Gauge

When the weather outside is frightful, this guy is so delightful!

what you'll need

*Foam balls, such as Styrofoam, in three
  different sizes*
Plastic knife
Wood craft stick
Fabric scraps
Buttons; paper clips; sticks
Small plastic cup
Small plastic plate
Scissors
Yardstick

now make it together

1 Using a plastic knife, saw off a small slice from the smallest and largest balls and two slices opposite each other on the medium-size ball.

2 Slide a wood craft stick through the center of the middle ball, leaving part of the stick coming through each flattened end. Poke the other two balls onto the stick, lining up the flattened edges.

3 Decorate the snowman as you like with scraps of fabric and buttons. Poke the buttons into the balls with a paper clip. Add stick arms.

4 To make the hat, push a small plastic cup into the top ball. Use a small plastic plate with the center cut out for the brim and add decorations. Push the bottom of the snowman onto the high-numbered end of the yardstick or meterstick. When there's a snowfall, stick the other end into the snow, and you'll see right away how deep the snow is.

**Talk With
Your Kids**
....
Look up
some trivia
on snow,
such as
what
regions
have snow
and where
the largest
measurable
amount was
recorded.

Happy New Year Crackers

Celebrate the new year with pop-open party favors that
are full of surprises.

what you'll need

*Paper towel tubes
Scissors; ruler
Wrapping paper; tape
Curling ribbon
Small candies*

now make it together

1 Make sure the paper towel tube is clean
inside and out. Cut tubes to measure
approximately 6 inches long; then cut each
tube in half.

2 Cut a piece of wrapping paper that is
11×6 inches. Center pieces of tube side
by side on paper, leaving a 1-inch space
between the tubes. Wrap paper around tubes
and secure with tape.

3 Tie one end of the paper with curling
ribbon. Fill the tube through the open
end with candy. Tie the remaining end shut.
Use scissors to curl the ends of the ribbon.

4 Have guests break tubes in half to find
goodies inside.

Glistening Goblets

Painted goblets double as elegant candleholders when filled with strings of beads and votive candles.

what you'll need
Clear glass stemware
Glass paint in desired colors
Disposable plate; paintbrushes
Strings of beads; votive candles

now make it together

1 Wash and dry the stemware. Avoid touching the areas to be painted.

2 Place small amounts of paint onto a disposable plate. Paint desired motifs on the base and stems of the glass. If layering colors, let dry between coats. Let the paint dry.

3 Bake the painted pieces in the oven if required by paint manufacturer. Let cool.

4 Place beaded string in the stemware. Nestle a votive candle in the beads. To avoid breakage, do not let the flame get close to the glass.

Note: For safety, never leave a burning candle unattended.

Talk With Your Kids
. . . .
Talk about all the wonderful things that happened in the past year and what you wish for the new one.

Hearty Bouquet

Go ahead—shower everyone with hearts and love with this endearing heart bouquet.

what you'll need

White and red air-dry clay, such as Crayola
  Model Magic clay
Green pencils
Green chenille stems
Green crafting foam scraps
Scissors; ribbon

now make it together

1 With your fingers, mix three parts white with one part red clay.

2 For each heart in your bouquet, roll out a 1-inch ball and make an indentation in the top. This will be the top of the heart.

3 Push the pencil's eraser into the bottom of the ball. Flatten and smooth the clay toward the top of the ball, forming the two rounded tops of the heart.

4 Roll out a small coil of white clay shaped in a heart. Lightly press the coil in place on the pink heart. Let air-dry overnight.

5 Cut leaf shapes out of crafting foam. Poke the end of a chenille stem through the leaf. Fold the stem over to hold leaf in place. Twist chenille stem around the pencil. Tie with ribbon.

Love Bugs

It's February—time for love bugs (that can be such shy bugs) to come out of hiding.

what you'll need

Wood hearts; paint or markers
Adhesive-backed jewelry pins
Wiggly eyes
Paper, felt, and crafting foam scraps
Scissors; sequins; small feathers; pom-poms
Thick white crafts glue

now make it together

1 Color hearts with paint or markers. Let dry.

2 From scraps, cut out and glue spots and wings to the heart body. Glue on wiggly eyes. Glue paper legs to underside and bend at knees. Cut and glue antennae. Decorate with desired trims. Let dry.

3 Remove paper backing from pin and attach to underside of bug. Cut out leaf-shape card; write message on leaf if desired. Pin bug to leaf.

Bright Idea
••••
Use double-sided tape to attach these enchanting insects to miniature bags of candy to make sweet gifts.

Sweet Cards

With a little cutting and pasting, you can make special valentine cards with a personalized message inside.

what you'll need

Construction paper
Ruler
Markers
Sucker, tea bag, and heart-shape
  balloon
Scissors; white glue
Transparent tape

now make it together

1 For each card, use a piece of construction paper approximately 7½×10 inches. Fold it in half.

2 FOR THE SUCKER CARD, cut out a red and white heart and glue to outside of card. Cut out two green leaves, draw veins, and glue. Make a loop of transparent tape and attach sucker to the card. Inside message: For my sweetheart.

3 FOR THE TEA BAG CARD, draw a tea cup, decorate it with markers, cut out, and glue to outside. Attach tea bag with loop of transparent tape. Inside message: You're my cup of tea.

4 FOR THE BALLOON CARD, cut out a yellow sun and white clouds. Glue them on the card. Attach the balloon with a loop of transparent tape. Inside message: Valentine, you blow me away.

Talk With Your Kids

Think of someone special who would appreciate a surprise handmade greeting.

Candy from Cupid

With sweet treats accompanying sweet sentiments, these valentine greetings are a double gift.

what you'll need

Colored paper; scissors
Markers
Paper punch
Flavor straw, such as Pixy Stix
Colored feathers
Tape

now make it together

1 Trace and cut out a heart from colored paper. See *pages 136–137* for a variety of heart patterns.

2 Write a message in the center of the heart with markers.

3 Punch a hole in the top of one side of the heart. Make another hole near the bottom of the heart.

4 Thread the flavor straw through the holes. Make sure it goes behind your message.

5 Tape two colored feathers to the top of the flavor straw.

6 Cut out a small paper heart and tape it to the bottom of the flavor straw.

Blooming Hearts

Send a flowerpot full of love with these cute paper-heart blooms.

Happy Valentines Day

I Love Yo[u]

To Mom

From Katie

what you'll need

Tracing paper; pencil; scissors
Colored paper in red, pink, purple, and green
Black marking pen
Paper fastener
Straws
Flowerpot; acrylic paint and brush, optional
Foam ball, such as Styrofoam
Conversation hearts; ribbon

now make it together

1 Trace the heart patterns, *below*. Cut out. Use patterns to cut large red, pink, and purple paper hearts for flowers and small hearts for leaves. Write messages on the large hearts as desired.

2 Stack three or four large hearts together. Pierce a paper fastener through the bottom and into the top of a straw. Do the same for the leaves.

3 Paint the flowerpot, if desired, and let it dry. Wedge foam ball into the flowerpot. Stick straws in the foam. Fill flowerpot with conversation hearts. Tie a ribbon bow around the top of the flowerpot.

LEAF HEART PATTERN

FLOWER HEART PATTERN

Heart Print Cards

Made from a child's handprints, these cards will be treasured for a lifetime.

what you'll need

Red and white acrylic paint
Paper plate
Paintbrush; red and white card stock
Paper
Ribbons
Red and opalescent glitter glue, optional
Paper punch
Scissors; glue stick

now make it together

1 Squeeze the paint out onto a paper plate and then brush it onto the outside of the child's hand along the pinky and palm. Have the child curl pinky to form the top of the heart. Gently help push hand onto the red paper to print half the heart. Repeat the process to the other hand and print the other side of the heart.

2 To make the full handprint heart, brush the paint over the whole palm and fingers. Print one hand; then apply paint to the other hand and line it up with the printed thumb and forefinger so the negative space makes a heart. To highlight the hearts, smudge a little glitter glue over them.

3 Cut out the finished heart prints and mount them onto folded card stock. Punch two holes on the sides and tie a ribbon through them.

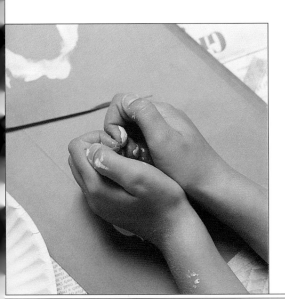

Talk With Your Kids
· · · ·
Tell your kids about the days they were born—how small their hands were and all the exciting events that surrounded their births.

**Bright
Idea**
····
Use this
idea to
make cards
for
birthdays,
anniversaries,
and
thank-yous.

Beaded Valentines

A wonderful beginning project for first-time
stitchers, these adorable cards will warm anyone's heart.

what you'll need

Letter beads
Embroidery floss; needle
Scissors; tracing paper; pencil
Felt in desired colors
Pinking shears
Card stock
Envelopes
Thick white crafts glue
Metallic marking pens in gold and silver

HEART PATTERN

now make it together

1 Decide what words you would like to put
on the card. Find those beads.

2 Thread the needle with three plies of
embroidery floss. Sew beads on felt,
leaving at least 2 inches on each side.

3 Trim felt with regular scissors or pinking
shears into a rectangle, heart, or other
desired shape. For heart patterns, see pattern
below or on *pages 136–137*. Trace pattern
onto tracing paper and cut out. If desired,
cut a second contrasting felt shape slightly
larger than the first. Glue together. Add a
background piece if desired. Glue together.

4 Cut and fold the card stock to the desired
size for the card. Glue the felt shape in
the center. Let the glue dry.

5 Add straight or dotted line borders using
metallic marking pens.

Watercolor Wishes

Say "I love you" with these beautiful heart embellished cards for Valentine's Day.

what you'll need

Watercolor paper; watercolor paints
Good medium round watercolor brush; salt
Scissors; glue stick
Air-dry clay, such as Crayola Model Magic clay
Rolling pin; heart cookie cutter
White pearl acrylic paint; paintbrush
White iridescent glitter
Fine gold wire
Tiny seed beads
Thick white crafts glue; ribbon

now make it together

1 Use a good quality watercolor paper in a manageable size. Soak watercolor paper thoroughly and lay on flat, smooth surface. Experiment with different paint color combinations. Magenta, purple, orange-yellow, and lime green were used on these.

2 When the water on the surface of the paper begins to soak in and before it dries is the best time to work with the paint. Fill round brush with concentrated color of paint. Brush, dot, or dabble onto wet surface as shown in Photo A, *below*. It should bleed as the brush touches surface. Before it dries, dabble on another color next to it so they bleed together. Continue to add colors. Paint in swirls if you wish. Work quickly so the paper doesn't dry.

3 When the paper is painted and surface is still visibly wet but not soaked, sprinkle lightly with salt where you want spotted texture as shown in Photo B. The salt will soak up the color from the paper. Let dry.

4 Brush dried salt off painting. Cut the painted paper into different sizes and shapes to use in creating your cards. Gather various colored papers together, layer, and glue coordinating colors, arranging into a card. Use a glue stick to adhere together

5 To make textured hearts, roll out clay to ⅛-inch thick. Cut out heart shapes with cookie cutter as shown in Photo C. Let dry.

6 Paint hearts with white pearl acrylic paint. Before the paint dries, sprinkle with white glitter.

7 String tiny, multicolored seed beads onto a length of wire to be placed behind the heart. Allow an area of no beads to fit behind heart.

8 Lay down wired beads and then glue the heart in place on top of the wire. Weigh it down with a heavy object until it dries, if necessary.

9 Add decorative ribbons loosely tied at the fold. Trim the ribbon ends.

Talk With Your Kids
....
Talk about Valentine's Day—how it started and the traditions you hold dear.

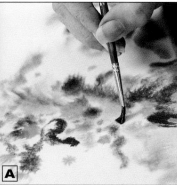

A

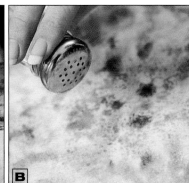

B

C

Flower-Topped Paperweight

This shining heart will be a reminder of sweet sentiments all year long.

what you'll need

Scissors
Waxed paper
Masking tape
Heart-shape cookie cutter
Plaster of Paris
Satin roses on stems
White map pins
Gems
Thick white crafts glue; paintbrush
Glitter in red and pink

now make it together

1 Cut a piece of waxed paper slightly larger than the heart cookie cutter. Tape the waxed paper firmly to the bottom of the cookie cutter. Place the cookie cutter on a smooth, hard work surface.

2 Mix approximately 1 cup of plaster. Pour into the cookie cutter, leaving about ⅛ inch empty at the top.

3 While the plaster is wet, add the decorations. To add satin flowers, cut the stems to approximately ¼ inch. Press into place. Add pins and gems as shown, *below.* Sprinkle between the decorations with red glitter. Let the plaster set.

4 Remove the tape and waxed paper. Paint the outside of the cookie cutter with glue. Sprinkle on pink glitter. Let dry.

Lacy Valentines

Your sweetheart will be all yours when presented with one of these lovely valentines.

what you'll need

Crocheted valentines or lace panel
Assorted card stock
Decoupage medium
Paintbrush; white pearl paint
Pinking shears; scissors
Decorative-edge scissors; glue stick
Colored foil; white paper

now make it together

1 For the lace panel valentine, trim any irregular edges off the lace. Lay it on card stock in a color you like. Paint a coat of decoupage medium over it. Let dry. Press under a heavy book after thoroughly dried if needed. Paint a coat of decoupage medium over the crocheted heart onto white paper. Let dry. Cut out the crocheted heart when dry. The crocheted heart can be painted a pearl white.

2 Trim the lace panel with pinking shears or scissors. Glue it to the front of a colored card. Glue the crocheted heart to the front of a card with the inside heart cut out. Place a foil panel inside the card to show through. Trim edges with decorative scissors.

Bright Idea
. . . .
Make a valentine tree by gathering fallen sticks. Paint them red. Fill a terra-cotta flowerpot with plaster. Arrange the sticks in the pot and let dry. Hang colored paper hearts from the branches.

Hugs 'n' Kisses Necklace

Tell friends how special they are with a necklace laden with hugs and kisses.

what you'll need

Nylon beading thread
Beading needle; yardstick
Large seed beads in white and red
Scissors

now make it together

1 Without cutting thread from spool, thread on groups of eight beads, alternating red and white. Continue stringing on beads until there are 15 groups of each color. Knot thread ends leaving one 36-inch tail of thread. Trim remaining thread.

2 With 36-inch thread in needle, push needle through several inches of beads, pushing needle out after two white beads as shown in Diagram A, *right*.

3 To make an X, work left to right. Thread seven red beads onto needle as shown in Diagram B. Push beads close to necklace. Skipping the last bead, push needle back through three beads as shown in Diagram C. Add three more red beads as shown in Diagram D. Skipping the last bead, push needle back through two beads and through the center bead. Add three more red beads. Attach to necklace by pushing the needle through two white necklace beads, as shown in Diagram E, and the next four red ones .

4 To make an O, thread 12 white beads on needle as shown in Diagram F. Push beads close to necklace. Push needle through first white bead, then through the remaining four red beads and two white beads on the necklace as shown in Diagram G.

5 Continue making Xs and Os in this manner until there are four red Xs and three white Os. Continue running thread through necklace beads until the thread ends can be knotted together. To hide thread ends, weave into beads in both directions. Trim thread ends.

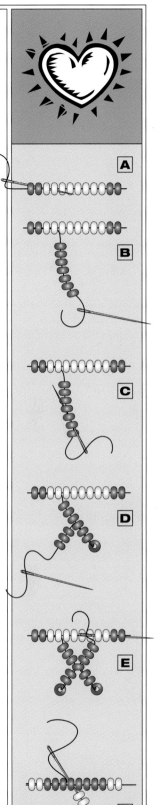

PICK-YOUR-SHAPE
HEART PATTERNS

Healthy Sips Soup Mug

Steaming soup will make anyone feel better, especially when served from this personalized mug!

what you'll need

Oven-safe soup mug or bowl
Ceramic paints in pink, purple, orange,
  green, aqua, or any other desired colors
Disposable plate
Fine liner and wide, flat paintbrushes

now make it together

1 Wash and dry the bowl or mug. Avoid touching the areas to be painted.

2 Place small amounts of paint onto a disposable plate. This paint dries very fast. Paint desired phrases in random directions, such as "get well, feel better, I love you," or any other sentiments. Use a wide, flat paintbrush to paint the wide letters and a fine liner brush to paint the thin letters. Let the paint dry.

3 Bake the painted piece in the oven if required by paint manufacturer. Let cool.

Bright Idea
• • • •
To make a basket for a child, include coloring books, crayons, a puppet, playing cards, and a handheld electronic game.

Get-Well Basket

Bring a basket of sunshine to someone who's feeling a bit under the weather.

what you'll need

Cloth place mat or large napkin
Large basket
Small basket to hold a soup can
Ribbon
Canned soup, flowers, and other get-well items

now make it together

1 Line the large basket with a cloth place mat or napkin. Place a can of soup in the smaller basket and tie the handles of the two baskets together using a generous length of ribbon.

2 Arrange the remaining items in the basket. Add an additional ribbon bow or two if desired.

Talk With Your Kids
····
Talk about favors you can do to help out neighbors when they're ill.

Feel-Better Blanket

As welcome as a bowl of warm soup, this cuddly blanket will have you feeling better in no time.

what you'll need

3 yards of yellow bias tape
35×54-inch piece of purple fleece
Yellow thread
Tracing paper
Pencil
Scissors
⅓ yard blue fleece
¼ yard yellow fleece
Fabric glue
25 small white pom-poms

now make it together

1 Aligning edges, machine-sew bias tape to the long sides of the purple fleece.

Trim threads. Cut 2-inch-long fringes on the short ends of the fleece.

2 Enlarge and trace the letters and star patterns, *pages 140–141.* Cut out the letter and star patterns. Use the patterns to cut enough letters from blue fleece to spell "Feel Better." Cut three small stars and two large stars from yellow fleece.

3 Using the placement guide, *pages 140–141,* glue the stars and letters to the right side of the fleece blanket. Glue pom-poms to the star tips. Let the glue dry.

1 SQUARE = 3 INCHES

spring

Bring on the brilliant palette and the freshness of spring with sunshiny projects the whole family will love making. You'll find oodles of creative ideas to celebrate the holidays of the new season, as well as cheerful flower and bug projects, pretty things to wear, and gifts that are sure smile winners.

crafting
in spring

As you gaze in awe at gently floating butterflies and ever-changing blooms, be inspired by all the beauty that unveils itself in spring. Use the glorious sights around you to boost your creativity when planning your next crafting adventure. Here we share some crafting secrets to help you capture the loveliness of the blossoming season to enjoy and share all year long.

- Keep a sketch pad with you on walks or drives. Draw flowers, bugs, or other signs of spring to incorporate into your crafting.

- Press and dry pretty seasonal flowers to use for floral arrangements, greeting cards, decoupage projects, or other crafts that need floral accents.

- Make a tabletop tree to celebrate every month of the year. Place short sticks into a container filled with plaster. Use the tree to display clay hearts, painted eggs, and paper shamrocks.

- Go on a basket-shopping spree—after Easter—to have on hand for putting together gift baskets throughout the year.

- Visit antiques stores and flea markets for glass candleholders in pastel colors. Group the holders together and top with colored eggs for a wonderful Easter arrangement.

- Start a rainy day fun box. Place crafting supplies in it to use when the weather keeps you in.

- Look for kites the next time you're in the toy department. Personalize one for each family member by painting favorite motifs using fabric paint.

- Plan a family outing to the local nursery. Let everyone pick out a flowerpot to decorate for the windowsill.

Spring is a great time to start a new journal. Purchase a plain one and embellish it with stamps, paint, ribbon, pressed flowers, or other crafts supplies.

When the school year comes to a close, sort through school papers and projects. Store the items in a plastic box and paint the lid with the year and other motifs using acrylic enamel paint.

Get out the water hose and wash the bikes and wagons. If needed, freshen up the items with a new coat of paint.

For a fun family project, plan a neighborhood garage sale. You'll clean the house, make some money, and may find bargains at your neighbors' to use in crafting.

Remember to show your affection on Mother's Day and Father's Day. A handcrafted labor of love will surely touch your loved ones' hearts.

Use fallen flowers, leaves, and rocks as stamps to make pretty gift wraps.

Use cone-shape cups to hold tiny May Day treasures. Paint and decorate the cups and use chenille stems for hangers.

Get ready for picnic time by personalizing a tablecloth and fabric napkins. Use fabric paints and sponges in desired shapes to add fun designs to the picnic cloths.

Recycle clear glass jars to use for holding spring blooms. Decorate the jars with gems, glass paint, or ribbons.

To celebrate the last day of school, make the teacher a special paperweight. Paint a rock using acrylic enamel paint. Let it dry. Glue a piece of felt on the bottom of the rock.

Prepare for summer sun by trimming a large-brimmed hat. Use scraps of felt to make flowers around a ribbon band. Add details using beads, pom-poms, and other crafts supplies.

Get ready for picnic weather! Visit a flea market or check out garage sales for baskets, lunch boxes, and other storage containers. Spruce them up with bright spray paint.

Flower-Sprinkled Umbrella

Chase rainy day frowns away with this sponge-painted umbrella.

what you'll need
Flat, expandable sponges (available at crafts stores)
Permanent black marking pen
Flower-shape cookie cutters, optional
Scissors; newspapers
Fabric paint pens in green, red, orange, and purple; umbrella

now make it together

1 Draw stem, leaf, and simple tulip, daffodil, and daisy shapes on flat sponges using marking pen. If desired, trace flower-shape cookie cutters for the motifs. Cut out the sponge shapes. Soak sponges in water to expand them; wring out.

2 Cover the work surface with newspaper. Squeeze green paint onto the stem sponge piece. Spread the paint evenly across the pattern using a scrap of sponge. Open the umbrella. Hold the stem sponge by its sides and press it on the fabric. Hold your other hand underneath the umbrella to add pressure.

3 Use the same method to apply green paint to the leaf pattern and apply to umbrella. Repeat using orange paint for tulips, red for daffodils, and purple for daisies. Or create your own color combinations. Let dry.

Bright Idea
....
Purchase alphabet stamps to write "Rain, Rain, Go Away" on your umbrella.

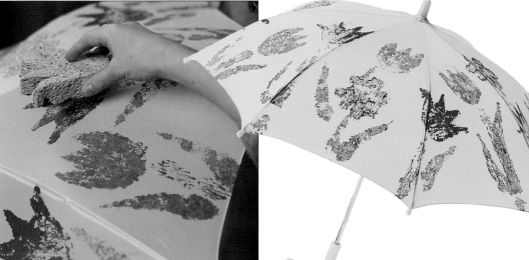

Color-Splashed Boots

Ready to wear or to hold a spring bouquet, these fun boots are splashed with vibrant colors of paint.

what you'll need
Rubber boots in desired color
Acrylic enamel paints in desired colors
Medium round paintbrush
Heavy drinking glass or metal can

now make it together

1 Using a paintbrush, apply a generous amount of paint around the top edge of each boot. Working with one color of paint at a time, apply enough paint so that it runs and drips. Let it dry before adding another color. Let the paint on the top dry before applying paint to the boot bottom.

2 Paint around the bottom edge as done for the top rim, holding boot upside down to allow the paint to run and drip. Rest the boot over a heavy drinking glass or can while it is drying.

3 Remove the boot from the glass or can and add random splashes, runs, and drips in desired paint colors. Let the paint dry.

Talk With Your Kids
. . . .
Talk about weather and what to expect in each season, such as when the first frost is or how many inches of rain usually fall annually.

**Bright
Idea**
• • • •
Use this
same idea
to make silly
gloves for
cold
weather
fun.

Bugs in a Box

Turn an old glove into a fistful of wiggly, giggly bugs!

what you'll need

Square tissue box
Scissors
Paints, markers, or stickers
Paintbrush
Colorful construction paper
Knit glove
Crafts glue
*Pom-poms, feathers, chenille stems, or other
  desired trim*
Wiggly eyes

now make it together

1 Cut a hole in the bottom of the tissue box. Paint the box or decorate it with markers or stickers.

2 Cut small faces out of paper. Glue them to the fingertips of the glove. Add details by gluing on feathers, pom-poms, and wiggly eyes. For antennae, push chenille stems through the fingertips and shape the ends.

3 Place your hand through the box, moving your fingers to make the bugs wiggle.

Dragonfly Barrettes

These beaded beauties will keep your locks in place when spring breezes blow.

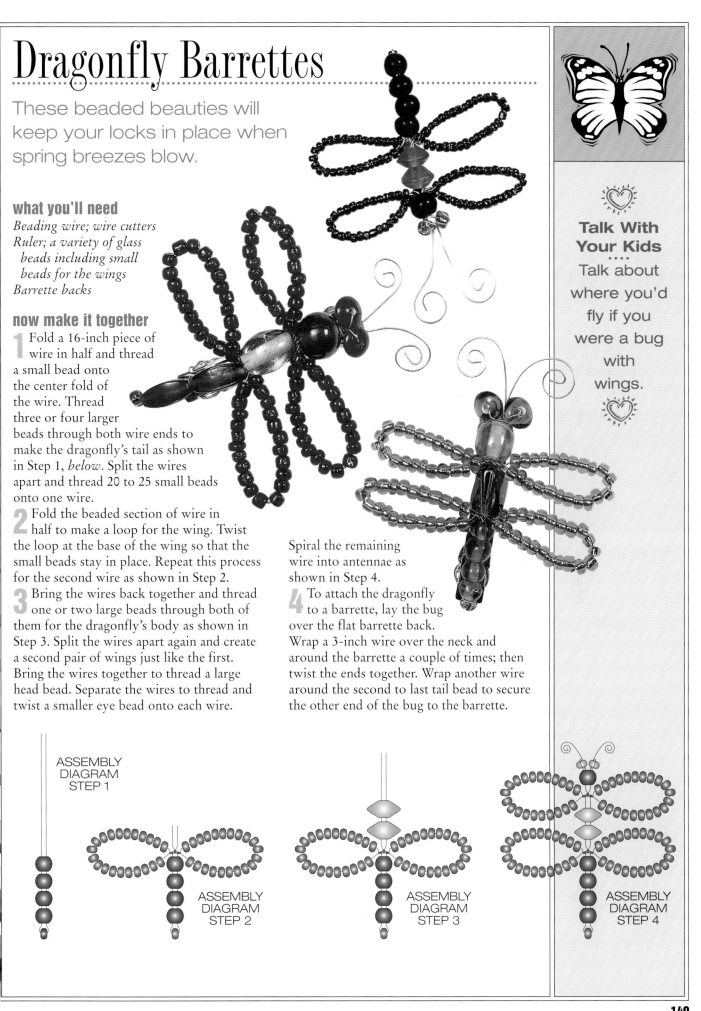

what you'll need

Beading wire; wire cutters
Ruler; a variety of glass
* beads including small*
* beads for the wings*
Barrette backs

now make it together

1 Fold a 16-inch piece of wire in half and thread a small bead onto the center fold of the wire. Thread three or four larger beads through both wire ends to make the dragonfly's tail as shown in Step 1, *below*. Split the wires apart and thread 20 to 25 small beads onto one wire.

2 Fold the beaded section of wire in half to make a loop for the wing. Twist the loop at the base of the wing so that the small beads stay in place. Repeat this process for the second wire as shown in Step 2.

3 Bring the wires back together and thread one or two large beads through both of them for the dragonfly's body as shown in Step 3. Split the wires apart again and create a second pair of wings just like the first. Bring the wires together to thread a large head bead. Separate the wires to thread and twist a smaller eye bead onto each wire.

Spiral the remaining wire into antennae as shown in Step 4.

4 To attach the dragonfly to a barrette, lay the bug over the flat barrette back. Wrap a 3-inch wire over the neck and around the barrette a couple of times; then twist the ends together. Wrap another wire around the second to last tail bead to secure the other end of the bug to the barrette.

Talk With Your Kids

Talk about where you'd fly if you were a bug with wings.

ASSEMBLY DIAGRAM STEP 1

ASSEMBLY DIAGRAM STEP 2

ASSEMBLY DIAGRAM STEP 3

ASSEMBLY DIAGRAM STEP 4

Poppin' Froggers

After the folding is done, have a great time seeing who can make their frogs jump the farthest!

what you'll need

3x5-inch index cards in bright colors
Marking pens, optional

now make it together

1 Place the index card on a flat surface. If desired, decorate the card with designs using marking pens.

2 Fold the top right corner of the card to the long edge at the left as shown in Diagram A, *left*. Crease it and unfold it. Fold the top left corner to the long edge at right as shown in Diagram B. Crease it and unfold it.

3 Turn the card over. Find the X formed by the creases (Diagram C). Make a crease across the middle of the X by folding the top corners down to the bottom corners of the X (Diagram D). Crease it and unfold it.

4 Turn the card back to the side you started with (Diagram E). It should be fully unfolded. Tuck in the edges you just folded so they touch each other as shown in Diagram F. This will form layers of triangles. Hold the bottom of the card in place.

5 Look at the top layer of the triangles. The tip is the frog's head. The two base points of the triangle will become the frog's front legs. Fold each base point up to the head (the tip) as shown in Diagram G.

6 Make the frog's body narrower. Fold each side in to meet at the centerline (Diagram H). Crease edges. Bring the center bottom of the body (the back legs) up to the tip of the head as shown in Diagram I. (The frog will spring better if you don't crease this.)

7 Fold the back legs down in half again as shown in Diagram J. Keep the fold loose.

8 To make the frog jump, pull the back legs out a little from the body. Then let your finger slide off the frog's back.

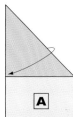 **A**

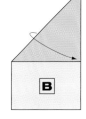 **B**

C

 **D**

E

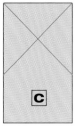 **F**

 **G**

 **H** **I** **J**

Lace Creatures

Putting on your sneakers will bring loads of giggles with these silly shoelace trims.

what you'll need

FOR THE BUTTERFLY:
Shoelaces
Crafting foam or felt
Scissors
Thick white crafts glue
Paper punch; ruler

FOR THE CATERPILLAR:
Shoelaces
6 pom beads; wiggly eyes
Chenille stems; scissors; ruler
Thick white crafts glue
Pencil

now make it together

1 FOR THE BUTTERFLY SHOELACES, cut two 2½-inch-wide butterflies from crafting foam. Decorate the wings with contrasting crafting foam scraps attached with glue.

2 Use a paper punch to place two holes in the middle of each butterfly. Place each of the shoelaces through the holes and move the butterflies to the center of the laces. Place the laces in shoes so the butterflies are perched on the bottom loop of the laced section.

3 FOR THE CATERPILLAR SHOELACES, use pom beads to turn laces into caterpillars. Pom beads are fuzzy pom-poms that can be used like beads. String three pom beads onto each shoelace.

4 Glue two wiggly eyes on the last pom bead of each lace. This is the caterpillar head. Curl a 2-inch piece of chenille stem around a pencil. Twist the curled stem between the head of the caterpillar and the pom bead next to it for the caterpillar's antennae. Tie laces into bow, drawing the pom beads together to form a caterpillar.

Talk With Your Kids
····
Buy a book about butterflies and learn how to tell species by the markings on their wings.

Crazy Paper Plate Pets

Let your imagination soar with crazy critters that can take any shape or form.

what you'll need

Paper plates
Marking pens
Tape
Construction paper
Scissors; ruler
Thick white crafts glue
Large wiggly eyes or black and
  white paper, tin cans or plastic lids,
  and a pencil
Pom-poms

now make it together

1 For each puppet, color both sides of a paper plate with marking pens (or start with a colored plate). Fold the plate in half.

2 Tape the edges of a 4×1½-inch paper strip on top of the plate for your fingers and a 2×1½-inch strip on the bottom for your thumb.

3 Cut out paper feathers, teeth, a tongue, background for eyes, antennae, and other desired features. Fold, bend, and curl the features as desired.

4 Arrange the paper features on the colored plate and glue in place. Let the glue dry.

5 Glue on the wiggly eyes. If you don't have eyes large enough for this project, cut out eyes from white and black paper. Use cans or plastic lids to trace around. Trace a large circle for the white eye and a smaller black circle for the pupil. Cut out. Glue the black circles to the bottom of the white circles or place the pupils in different places to create various expressions. Glue on pom-poms for the nostrils. Experiment with different shapes to make the creatures look scared, happy, or terrifying. Let the glue dry.

Chirping Cricket

Kids will have a leapin' good time making their crickets chirp.

what you'll need

Cardboard tube; scissors; green acrylic paint
Paintbrush; tracing paper; pencil
Craft foam scraps; craft sticks; chenille stem
Emery board; paper punch; 2 pom-poms
2 wiggly eyes; thick white crafts glue

now make it together

1 Cut off a diagonal wedge from one end of the tube to shape the tail. Cut a mouth shape on the bottom of the other end of the tube. Paint the tube green and let it dry.

2 Trace the patterns. Use patterns to cut a pair of back legs and arms out of craft foam. Glue the arms under the cricket behind the mouth. Glue the legs to each side of the tube in front of the tail. Glue an emery board or notched craft stick to the cricket's legs.

3 Punch two holes on top of the tube for antennae. Fold the chenille stem in half and thread the ends through the holes. Glue the pom-poms to the tube rim. Glue wiggly eyes to the pom-poms. To make the cricket chirp, rub a craft stick across the textured surface on the legs.

LEG PATTERN

ARM PATTERN

Party Favor Centerpiece

Inexpensive party favors make a playful centerpiece at your next birthday gala.

Bright Idea

····

Turn this centerpiece idea into a two-in-one gift by placing a pair of goldfish in the glass bowl.

what you'll need

12-inch wreath foam, such as Styrofoam
7 yards of 1½-inch-wide grosgrain ribbon
Inexpensive party favors
Hot-glue gun and hot-glue sticks
Glass bowl
Ribbon
Scissors
Jelly beans or other desired candies

now make it together

1 Placing the ribbon at a slight angle, wrap the entire wreath with the ribbon. Begin and end on the back side. Glue the loose ends to the back.

2 Hot-glue party favors randomly to the front of the wreath.

3 Place a glass bowl in the center of the ring. Fill with candy or other party goodies. Tie a ribbon around the lip of the bowl. Fill the bowl with candies.

Pinwheel Party Wreath

Get the party off to a festive start with this whimsical wreath to greet your guests.

what you'll need

6 inches of 18-gauge wire
Thick white crafts glue
16-inch wreath foam, such as Styrofoam
2 yards of tulle netting in desired color
5 large metallic pinwheels
Awl; ruler
3 small metallic pinwheels
Metallic curling ribbons
Scissors
Flathead pins

now make it together

1 Bend wire in half to form a loop. Twist ends together. Add glue to the ends and push them into the back of the wreath for a hanger.

2 Cut tulle into 6-inch-wide strips. Wrap the tulle around the wreath form, pinning the ends of the tulle to the back side of the wreath.

3 Remove handles from the five large pinwheels. Push the ends of the pinwheels into the top edge of the wreath, arranging the pinwheels evenly across the top of the wreath. If necessary, use an awl to make a hole in the foam first.

4 Trim the handles on the smaller pinwheels to measure about 6 inches in length. Push them into the top edge of the wreath bottom as shown, *above*.

5 Pin lengths of curling ribbon to the wreath under the edges of the pinwheels. Trim as desired.

Talk With
Your Kids
. . . .
Talk about
the most
memorable
parties
you've
attended.

Egg Flowers

Everlasting paper blooms can be made in all the colors of spring.

what you'll need
Cardboard tubes
Construction paper
Pencil
Scissors
Thick white crafts glue
Rubber bands
Dyed or decorated Easter eggs

now make it together

1 Draw a flower on colored construction paper. Trace the tube end onto the middle of the flower.

2 Poke hole in center of circle. Create flaps for attaching flowers to tube by making small cuts from the center hole to the edge of the circle. Bend up flaps.

3 Glue flaps to outside of the tube. Glue green construction paper around tube, using rubber bands to secure until dry. Remove rubber bands. Cut leaves and glue to tube. Place a colored egg in the top of the tube.

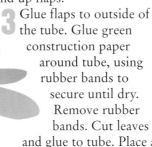
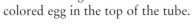

Egg Rabbit

Put these bunnies in Easter baskets and there will be lots of smiles.

what you'll need
Tracing paper
Pencil
Foam egg, such as Styrofoam; felt scraps
Chenille stem; pom-poms
Thick white crafts glue
Colored straight pins; ribbon; scissors

now make it together

1 Trace the patterns, *below.* Use patterns to cut pieces from felt. Glue pieces to egg.

2 Poke pins through both felt and foam egg for eyes. Add felt trim to ears.

3 Glue on pom-pom nose and tail. Poke in chenille stem whiskers. Tie a bow with ribbon and glue it under the neck.

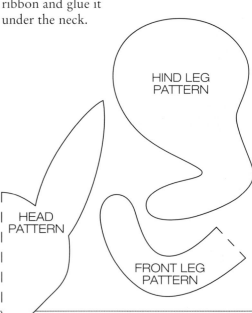

HIND LEG PATTERN

HEAD PATTERN

FRONT LEG PATTERN

Thread Eggs

If stored carefully, these delicate see-through eggs can be used for years.

what you'll need

Small oval balloons; pin
Scissors; embroidery floss or sewing thread
Liquid starch or fabric stiffener; ruler

now make it together

1 Inflate small balloons and tie the necks tightly.

2 Soak 12- to 24-inch lengths of embroidery floss or thread (use one color or a variety of colors) in liquid starch or fabric stiffener. Soak each piece of floss separately and pull the wet thread between your thumb and forefinger to remove excess liquid.

3 Wrap the wet threads around the balloon one at a time. The thread will stick to the balloon without any additional glue or fastener. Cover the balloon by crisscrossing the threads any way you choose. Use less thread for an open, lacy egg, or wrap additional thread for an egg that looks more solid.

4 Tie a piece of dry thread around the neck of the thread-wrapped balloon and hang it until the thread is dry and hard to the touch. Pop the balloon with a pin and pull the balloon out of the top of the egg shape. Place the eggs in a basket or attach loops of floss so they can be hung on a tree branch to create an egg tree.

Easter Hat

Don your spring bonnet for an "eggstravagant" time!

what you'll need

Heavyweight tissue paper or colored paper
¾-inch masking tape
Double-sided tape; thick white crafts glue
Silk flowers; purchased foam eggs

now make it together

1 Place paper over a child's head and wrap masking tape around the brim. Roll the corners toward the center, securing the edges with double-sided tape.

2 Glue silk flowers and foam eggs on one side of the hat. Let the glue dry.

Stars and Stripes Eggs

Dyed in Easter's pastel hues, these eggs are created with star stickers and rubber bands.

what you'll need

Hard-boiled or blown-out eggs
Commercial egg dye or food coloring
Star stickers
Rubber bands

now make it together

1 Prepare the egg dye as instructed on the package or use food coloring to dye the eggs. Set aside.

2 To make the star eggs, press star stickers on the undyed eggs. Rub carefully around the edges of the stickers. Dip the eggs in the dye. Let the dye dry. Remove the stickers.

3 To make the striped eggs, wrap rubber bands around the eggs, using wide rubber bands or combining more than one rubber band. Dip the eggs in the dye. Let the dye dry. Remove the rubber bands.

Glittery Eggs

To make elegant eggs, let them glisten with a glaze of glitter fingernail polish and then add accents of tiny metallic beads.

what you'll need
Plaster or wood eggs
Bright colored acrylic paint
Paintbrush
Assorted glitter nail polishes
Fabric paint pen
Small glass or metallic beads
Vintage bowl

now make it together

1 Paint the eggs using acrylic paint. Let the paint dry. Apply a second coat if needed. Let dry.

2 To add glitter effect, apply nail polish over the eggs as shown in Photo A, *below.* Experiment with different color combinations. Here, green, aqua, purple, and pink nail polishes were used over the magenta egg; lime green and aqua polishes were used over the green egg; orange and pink polishes were used over the yellow egg. Let the nail polish dry.

3 Decorate the egg surface as desired using fabric paint as shown in Photo B. Add swirls, lines, zigzags, or any other shapes. Add fabric paint to one side at a time. Place beads in wet paint as shown in Photo C. Let the paint dry. Turn the egg over and decorate the remaining side. Let the paint dry.

4 To display the eggs, arrange them in a vintage bowl.

Talk With Your Kids
····
What are your favorite colors? What colors make you feel happy, calm, or excited?

**Bright
Idea**
····
Use wood
or plaster
eggs to
keep these
painted
eggs from
year to
year.

"Eggceptional" Eggs

Gather pencils, a toothbrush, adhesive bandages, and toothpicks and you're ready to decorate eggs!

what you'll need

Hard-boiled eggs
Cardboard paper towel tube
Masking tape
Acrylic paint in desired colors; paintbrush
Disposable plate
Toothbrush
Toothpicks
Pencil with new eraser
Adhesive bandages; scissors

now make it together

1 If you want the background color to be the natural white (or brown) of the eggshell, just decorate a plain egg. For other colors, paint the egg a solid color and let it dry. To keep the egg from rolling, cut a short section from a paper towel tube and tape to the table.

2 FOR THE TOOTHBRUSH (MARBLEIZED) TECHNIQUE, pour some paint onto a

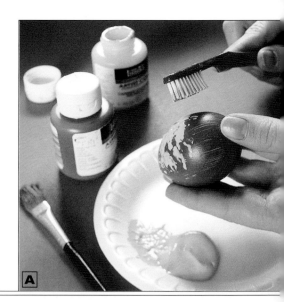

A

B

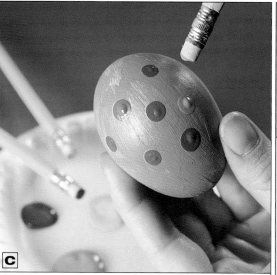

C

plate. Dip the end of the toothbrush bristles into the paint and dot the egg as shown in Photo A, *opposite.* Let one side dry; then repeat on the other side. Let dry.

3 FOR THE TOOTHPICK (FLOWER) TECHNIQUE, choose two colors of paint to decorate your egg and pour those paints on the disposable plate. To make the petals of the flower, dip about ¼ inch of the toothpick into the paint; then lay the toothpick down onto the egg, making a petal as shown in Photo B, *above.* Repeat making petals in a circle as shown on the floral egg, *opposite,* leaving a space in the middle for the flower center. Work on one side of the egg at a time. Let the paint dry. Repeat on the other side. Using a new toothpick and another color of paint, dip just the tip of the toothpick in the paint and dot the center two or three times. Let the paint dry.

4 FOR THE PENCIL ERASER (SPOTTED) TECHNIQUE, pour some paint onto a disposable plate. Dip the end of the eraser

into the paint and dot the egg as shown in Photo C, *above right.* Paint the dots using the desired colors. Dot on one color at a time. Wash or wipe off the eraser before changing colors. Work on one side of the egg at a time, overlapping the dots if desired. Let dry. Repeat on the other side.

5 FOR THE ADHESIVE BANDAGES (STRIPED) TECHNIQUE, leave the egg natural; do not paint. Cut larger bandages in half lengthwise or use small bandages to decorate the egg. Overlap the bandage strips as shown, Photo D, or make whatever design you choose. Working on one side of the egg at a time, paint the egg. Let the paint dry. Repeat on the other side, covering all of the bandages. Try to keep the paint from running underneath the bandage edges. Let the egg dry. Carefully peel off the adhesive bandages as shown in Photo E, *below.* There will be eggshell-colored stripes where the bandages were placed.

Talk With Your Kids
. . . .
Talk about the proper handling of eggs and different ways they can be cooked.

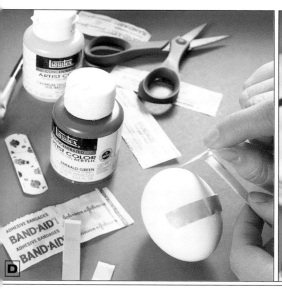

D

E

Cross-Stitch Trinket Box

A great beginner's project, this cheerful cross-stitched nature box can hide the tiniest treasures.

what you'll need

Scissors; tape
7-count plastic canvas; ruler
Cotton embroidery floss in
  colors listed in key
Needle; Heat 'n' Bond; iron

now make it together

1 Cut six 22×22-hole pieces of plastic canvas (this measures approximately 3⅜×3⅜ inches). Trim away rough edges so thread does not catch on border as you stitch.

2 Thread needle with a double strand of floss. Draw ends of thread together and tape down on back side of canvas near beginning of stitch area. The taping will control thread for beginners better than trying to hold down thread while stitching.

3 Find the center of one chart and the center of one square of canvas. Work desired number of half cross-stitches in one direction; then complete cross-stitch by working back over half cross-stitches. Be sure to work over taped end of thread to tack in place.

4 When area is completed or thread becomes short, run needle under a few stitches on the back side of the canvas to tack down. Cut thread end. Continue working until design is completed.

5 For border, use the background floss color to whipstitch across the outside edge in one direction; then work back across in opposite direction. Work two whipstitches in each corner hole. Tack ends.

6 For finishing, cut six 3¼×3¼-inch pieces of felt and six 3¼×3¼-inch pieces of Heat 'n' Bond. Bond backing to felt as directed. To bond felt to cross-stitch piece, place on wrong side of canvas, use steam setting on iron to penetrate felt, and hold for 10 seconds.

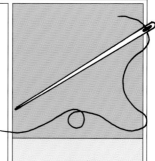

7 To assemble box, lay out squares and arrange in desired pattern. Using two strands of coordinating floss, place two squares with right sides facing. Whipstitch sides together. Repeat until all four side pieces are joined in a row. Form a square by bringing the ends together with right sides facing out. Sew together with blind stitches. Blindstitch base to bottom of squares, and whipstitch lid on outside of design.

Anchor		DMC	
002	•	000	White
403	■	310	Black
371	⊞	433	Chestnut
046	✕	666	True red
256	I	704	Chartreuse
304	+	741	Tangerine
054	▽	956	Geranium
297	−	973	True canary
100	▲	3837	Lavender
1089	○	3845	Turquoise

BACKSTITCH

403	╱	310 Black – antennae on butterfly
403	╱	433 Chestnut – bird

WHIPSTITCH DIAGRAMS

BLIND STITCH
DIAGRAM

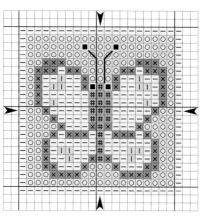
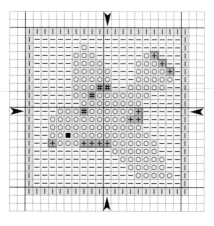
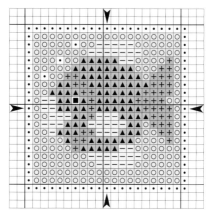
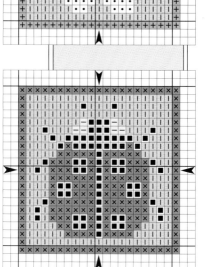

Perk-Me-Up Barrettes

When you want to pull back your hair during sun-kissed weather, these pretty hair trims are the perfect finishing touch for springtime dress.

Chenille Stem Barrette

what you'll need

1-inch peach button
5/8-inch yellow button
3/8-inch pink button
Thin chenille stems in purple, orange, and yellow
Regular chenille stems in pink and green
Ice pick; hot-glue gun and hot-glue sticks
Barrette back

now make it together

1 Stack the buttons with the largest on the bottom. From the bottom, push a purple chenille stem through a hole in each button. Slide buttons to the center of the chenille stem. Poke the end of the chenille stem back through the remaining hole. If the buttons have four holes, repeat the process.

2 Fold the pink, orange, and yellow chenille stems in half. Secure the folds to the purple chenille stem just under the large button using the green chenille stem.

3 Shape the ends of the green chenille stem into leaves. Wrap the remaining chenille stems around an ice pick to curl.

4 Hot-glue the decoration to a barrette back. Let it dry.

Bow Barrette

what you'll need

1½-inch ribbon; barrette back
Scissors; flat marble
Hot-glue gun and hot-glue sticks

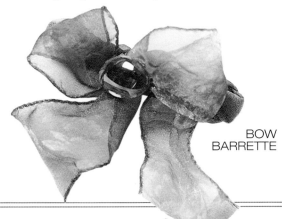

BOW BARRETTE

now make it together

1 Wrap ribbon around the barrette top until covered. Glue ends on the back side. Slip another piece of ribbon under the center wraps. Tie into a bow.

2 Glue a marble in the center of the bow. Trim the ribbon ends.

RIBBON
BARRETTE

Ribbon Barrette

what you'll need

⅛-inch satin ribbons; ruler
Barrette back
Scissors

now make it together

1 Cut ribbons into 5-inch lengths. Tie around barrette top, knotting to secure. Continue adding ribbons until barrette top is covered. Trim ribbon ends if necessary.

Butterfly Barrette

what you'll need

Barrette back
Silicone glue
Artificial butterfly

now make it together

1 Decide how to place the butterfly on the barrette.

2 Put a line of glue along the barrette, being careful not to get any on the hinge. Gently press the butterfly in place. Let the glue dry.

JEWELED
BARRETTE

Jeweled Barrette

what you'll need

Pliers
Clip earrings
Emery board
Hot-glue gun and hot-glue sticks
Barrette back

now make it together

1 Using pliers, remove the clips from the earrings. Sand any rough edges using an emery board.

2 Arrange and glue the earrings to the barrette top. Let the glue dry.

Talk With Your Kids

....

Talk about the many hair styles you've had throughout the years. Find photos to show each style.

BUTTERFLY
BARRETTE

Bright Idea
....
Use this jewelry technique to make trims for lampshades.

Sea Glass Jewelry

Whether you live inland or right by the shore, this sparkling jewelry will capture your heart.

what you'll need

Sea glass
Gold wire; jump rings
Leather cord
Lobster claw clasp
Fish hook earring findings
1-inch-long eye pins
Frosted glass beads
Needle-nose pliers
Wire cutters; ruler

now make it together

1 Wrap each piece of glass with 6-inch piece of wire, carefully trapping the glass on all sides. Tightly twist the wire ends together; then cut away the extra wire. Fold the twisted wire end flat against the glass.

2 TO MAKE A PENDANT, thread a jump ring through the wrapping wire and crimp the jump ring closed with the pliers. Thread a leather cord through the jump ring and knot the cord ends together.

3 TO MAKE EARRINGS, thread the ring end of an eye pin through the wrapping wire. Thread several glass beads onto the straight section of the pin, followed by the ring end of the fish hook earring finding. Use the pliers to bend over the wire end. The beads and glass should dangle freely from the hook of your finished earring. Repeat the process with matching beads and a similar piece of glass to make the second earring.

4 TO MAKE A BRACELET, connect wrapped pieces of glass with small sections of wire threaded with glass beads. Thread the wire ends of the small sections through the wrapping wire, loop them over, and twist them closed. To one side of the bracelet, attach a small section of wire with a lobster claw clasp looped onto the end. To the other side add a section of wire that ends in a loop twisted shut. These two ends will allow the bracelet to fasten and unfasten.

Pretty Posy Pins

These pretty corsages make a great gift and are just right to wear on a special occasion.

what you'll need

Bunches of tiny fabric flowers
Fabric leaves on wire stems
Utility scissors; ruler
Green florist's tape
2-inch piece of ¼-inch-wide balsa wood
1½-inch-long pin back
Thick white crafts glue

now make it together

1 Separate the flower bunches. Choose a few favorite flowers to make the corsage. Arrange two or three leaves with the flowers. Trim the flower and leaf stems to measure approximately 2 inches long. Wrap the stems with florist's tape as shown in Photo A, *right.* After wrapping the bottom of the stems, wrap back up to the top. Trim the tape.

2 Wrap the tiny piece of balsa wood with florist's tape as shown in Photo B.

3 Using florist's tape, wrap the wood piece to the flower bunch as shown in Photo C.

4 Glue the back of the pin to the back side of the wrapped stems and balsa wood as shown in Photo D. Let the glue dry.

Blooming Place Mats

Make every meal a special event with these colorful mats gracing the table.

what you'll need

Pencil
Tracing paper
Scissors
Crafting foam in white, yellow, green,
 and red-pink
Green chenille stems
Silicone glue
Foam place mats in desired colors

now make it together

1 Trace the patterns, *pages 171–173*. Cut out. Trace around pattern pieces on coordinating pieces of crafting foam. Cut out shapes.

2 Bend chenille stems into desired shape for stems. Glue in place on foam place mat, bending ends to the mat back.

3 Using the photo, *below*, as a guide, glue the foam pieces in place to make flowers. Add leaves. Let the glue dry.

Springtime Napkin Rings

So easy to do, you can braid up a table full of these pretty napkin rings in an evening.

Bright Idea
· · · ·
Use a roll of woven foam drawer liner to make a table runner similar to these place mats. .

what you'll need

3 colors of chenille stems
Paper towel tube; ruler

now make it together

1 Choose six chenille stems, two of each color. Even up the ends of chenille stems, grouping colors. Leaving 3 inches at one end, begin to braid the chenille stems. Stop braiding 3 inches from the opposite end.

2 For looped ends, bend over the chenille stems to form loops. Secure by wrapping a separate chenille stem around the ends. Tuck end of chenille stem into wraps.

3 For wrapped ends, braid entire length of six chenille stems. Wrap ends tightly with a separate chenille stem.

4 To shape, wrap braided chenille stems around a paper tube.

BLOOMING
PLACE MATS
WHITE FLOWER
PATTERN

Talk With
Your Kids
• • • •
Discuss
your favorite
flowers.
Which are
the prettiest
and which
have the
best scent?

patterns continued on pages 172–173

Bright Idea
· · · ·
Use these flower patterns to add designs to all sorts of things, such as posters, pillows, and gift boxes.

BLOOMING
PLACE MATS
YELLOW FLOWER
PATTERN

BLOOMING
PLACE MATS
RED-PINK FLOWER
PATTERN

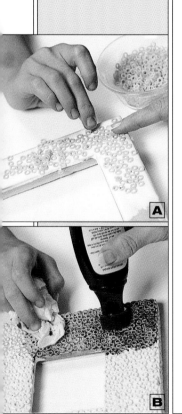

A

B

Pasta Frames

Wonderful for framing favorite photos or little ones' works of art, these fun frames can be whipped up with few supplies, some from the kitchen cupboard!

what you'll need

Frame with wide flat surface
Thick white crafts glue
Pasta of your choice, rings, or couscous
Cream-colored acrylic paint
Paintbrush
Shoe polish in blue or brown
Rag
Clear varnish or sealer
Newspaper

now make it together

1 Remove glass and backing from frame. Lay frame flat on paper-covered work surface. Spread an even, generous layer of glue onto surface of frame you wish to texturize. Sprinkle or arrange the pasta onto the wet glue as shown in Photo A, *left.* Let the glue dry.

2 Paint the entire frame with cream-colored acrylic paint. Let the paint dry. Paint another coat if necessary. Let the paint dry.

3 Coat the entire frame with shoe polish in blue or brown as shown in Photo B. Dab off extra shoe polish with a rag, wiping enough off to leave the raised area a light color and the crevices a deeper color. Let the polish dry.

4 Paint a coat of clear varnish or sealer over entire frame. Let it dry.

Block Frames

Simple art on small blocks creates clever frames to feature a special child.

what you'll need

Two ¾-inch wood blocks
One 2-inch wood block
Two 4-inch squares of windowpane glass
(ask the frame store to buff the edges so you are less likely to cut yourself)
Acrylic paints in a variety of colors
Small paintbrushes
Wood glue
Clear acrylic spray sealer
Epoxy glue
4 marbles

now make it together

1 Glue the ¾-inch blocks on the top of the 2-inch block, ¼ inch apart, centered on the top of the 2-inch block. Base-coat the blocks as desired.

2 Dip a thumb in some paint to create the base of the flower or the bee. Make wings, stinger, head, stripes, and antennae in black to complete the bee. Add petals, stem, leaves, and grass to complete the flower. Embellish with lines of polka dots. Let dry.

3 Spray the painted block with clear acrylic sealer and let dry.

4 Glue the marbles on the bottom of large wood block as shown, *below,* with the epoxy glue. Let dry.

5 Place a photo between the glass and slide between the small blocks. Display two photos if desired.

Talk With Your Kids
····
Talk about your favorite photos and why they are special to you.

Vintage Linen Picture Mats

Perfect for Mother's Day gifts, vintage picture mats are inspired by the alluring and vibrant linens of the '40s and '50s.

what you'll need

Various sizes of acrylic frames
Several vintage tablecloths, tea towels,
 or napkins
Masking tape
Ruler
Color copier
Scissors
Crafts knife
Photograph

now make it together

1 Select the size frame you will be using. Select the linen you like best and mask off an area that measures the size of your frame. For example, on an 8×10 frame, mask off a 10×12 area that features the images on the linen that you like best.

2 Take the linen to a color copier and make copies. Be sure to tell the copier assistant to keep the colors bright.

3 With scissors, cut the copied image to fit the size of your frame. Use a crafts knife to cut out an opening in which you will feature a photograph.

4 Tape the photograph so that the image appears in the cut opening of the copied linen. Slide it into the acrylic frame.

Bright Idea
••••
Make wrapping paper by photocopying favorite vintage linens.

Talk With Your Kids
....
Make a tote bag that stays in the family car. Store items you want to have on hand while traveling.

Mom's Tote Bag

Mom will love this sturdy fringed tote that is as pretty as it is practical.

what you'll need
*Braided or chenille fringed rug,
  approximately 20×30 inches
Matching thread
Heavy braid or decorative rope
Scissors; heavy-duty hand sewing needle
Heavy-duty nylon thread
Yardstick*

now make it together

1 Fold a rug in half with the short fringed ends together. Machine-sew each side seam. Do not turn. Fold the top fringed end over to create a 3-inch cuff.

2 To make a handle, cut a 40-inch piece of heavy braid, allowing for 5 inches of braid to be sewn onto each side. Thread a hand sewing needle with heavy-duty nylon thread. Sew one end of handle to one inside side seam approximately 5 inches from purse top. Secure with several stitches. Repeat for the opposite end of the handle.

3 Make a tuck on each side of purse. Fold the outside seam inward about 2½ inches. Hand-sew the tuck in place along the outside edge.

Clever Magnetic Frames

There will always be smiles in the kitchen with these colorful frames holding Mom's treasured snapshots in place on the refrigerator door.

what you'll need
Scissors
Crafting foam
Self-adhesive notes
Glitter glue
Pom-poms
Plastic gemstones
Silk or plastic cord
Other desired trims
Craft glue or hot-glue gun and hot-glue sticks
Adhesive magnet strips
Card stock; tape

now make it together

1 Cut a rectangle out of crafting foam. Stick a self-adhesive note to the center of the rectangle. Trace around the self-adhesive note with a pen and then remove the paper.

2 Carefully cut along the lines to remove the center of the frame. Stick strips of adhesive magnet on the wrong side of the photo frame.

3 Turn the crafting foam over and decorate it with glitter glue, pom-poms, plastic gemstones, silk, or plastic cord, or other trims using the photographs, *above*, for inspiration. Let the glue dry.

4 Fold the card stock in half and write a message on the inside. Stick tape loops on the back of the frame between the magnet strips to stick it to the front of the card.

Talk With Your Kids
••••
Share your favorite stories and make magnetic characters to act out the stories.

Jack-and-Jill Magnetic Storyboard Figures

Hours of fun await on the refrigerator for Mom, Dad, and kids with these ready-to-play storybook characters.

what you'll need

Pencil
Tracing paper
Scissors
White magnetic register vent cover material
  (available at hardware stores)
Permanent black marking pen
Acrylic paints in desired colors
Paintbrushes
Slick tube paints

now make it together

1 With a pencil, trace the patterns from *pages 180–181* onto tracing paper. Cut out. Draw around the pattern onto the magnetic sheet. Transfer all the details.

2 Use acrylic paint in desired colors to paint clothing for Jack and Jill, the hill, clouds, well, pail, and flowers. Let the paint dry.

3 Use a black marking pen to outline the figures, clothing details, and to add facial features.

4 Cut all figures out with scissors. Use the slick paint to add polka dots and stripes.

Bright Idea
····
Make the shapes from felt to play with in the car.

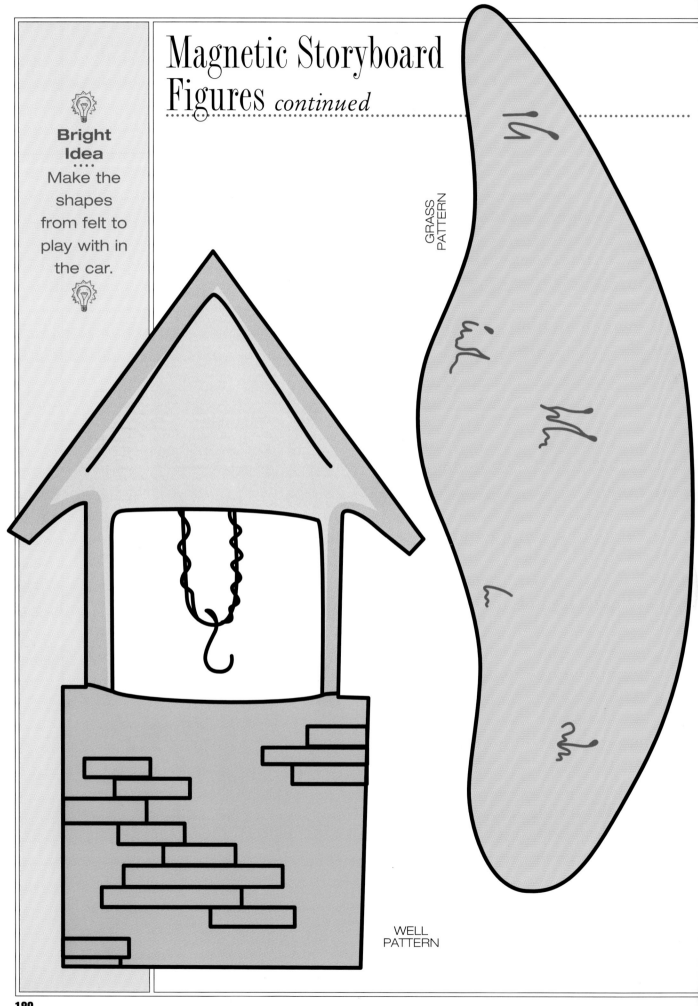

GRASS PATTERN

WELL
PATTERN

JILL
PATTERN

FLOWER
PATTERN

SMALL
CLOUD
PATTERN

LARGE
CLOUD
PATTERN

PAIL
PATTERN

JACK
PATTERN

Charm Cards

These charming Mother's Day necklaces do double duty as endearing greeting cards. For even more fun, try making a charm to resemble each family member.

what you'll need
Thin chenille stems
Jump ring
Wood beads
¼-inch ribbon
Metal ball chain
Card stock
Scissors
Ruler
Glue stick
Decorative papers
Tape

now make it together

1 Fold a chenille stem in half. Thread a jump ring onto the center of the chenille stem. Thread both ends of the chenille stem through the wood bead head.

2 Bend each of the chenille stems out at a 90-degree angle to make the arms approximately ¾-inch long. Fold the stems back along the arms until they meet at the body. Twist the stem together once and then form the remaining ends into a triangle skirt for the girl or inch-long legs that fold back

onto themselves for the boy. In either case, twist the ends together and trim away the leftover chenille stem. Make as many boy or girl charms as desired.

3 Tie a small bow around the waists of the girl charms. Thread the appropriate combination of girl or boy charms onto the metal ball chain.

4 To make a card, fold a 5×8-inch piece of card stock in half and then glue one or two rectangles of decorative paper to the front of the card. Make two small slits in the top of the card and then thread each end of the necklace through the slits. Clasp the necklace behind the card; then wind up the extra ball chain and loosely tape it behind the front of the card.

Symbols of Spring Soap

With the variety of stickers available, you'll have fun finding Mom's favorites to make these handy soaps.

what you'll need

Colorful soap with smooth surface
Stickers; thick white crafts glue
Paraffin wax
Double boiler
Water

now make it together

1 Unwrap purchased soap. Smooth rough areas by wetting with water and smoothing with fingers. Let dry.

2 Affix stickers to top of soap as desired. Use thick white crafts glue if necessary to help stickers affix to soap.

3 Fill bottom of double boiler halfway with water. Place pan over water and place on stove. Melt paraffin wax in top of double boiler. Carefully remove pan of wax. Set on protected work surface. Dip the stickered surface only into the wax. The wax must be melted and hot or the coverage will be too thick. Turn soap right side up and let it cool.

Feather Pens

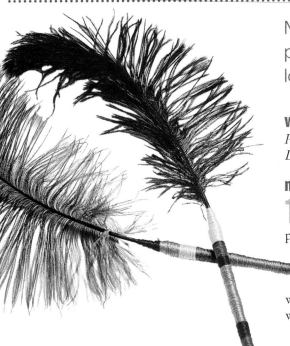

Mom will love these fancy pens for sending wishes of love to family and friends.

what you'll need

Pens; thick white crafts glue
Large feather plumes; cotton embroidery floss

now make it together

1 Remove the plug from the end of the pen. Glue a feather into the end of the pen. Let it dry.

2 Beginning just below the feather, wind the pen with floss, gluing as you go. Change colors when desired, being sure to secure floss ends with glue.

Talk With Your Kids
....
Talk about the history of writing tools. Let the kids try a pen dipped in ink.

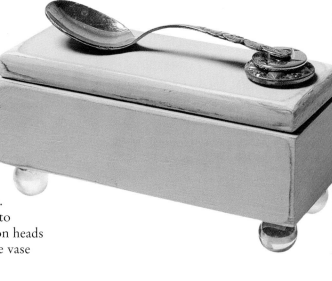

Teaspoon Vase

Silverware isn't just for mealtime anymore! Make these projects for Mom using flea market finds.

what you'll need

4 teaspoons
Hammer
2 thick towels
Clear 1½-inch diameter bud vase
Epoxy glue
Masking tape

now make it together

1 Hammer and beat the rounded spoon flat. Place the spoon in between two thick towels to eliminate damage to the work surface.

2 Bend the spoons at the base of the handle at a 90-degree angle.

3 Epoxy the handles of the spoons to the bud vase so the flattened spoon heads lay flat on the table. Tape them to the vase until the epoxy is dry. Remove tape.

Spoon-Handle Box

Everyone can use a little extra storage space, and this little beauty will be just right for helping Mom organize her trinkets.

what you'll need

5×2×2-inch wood box (available at crafts stores)
Acrylic paint; paintbrush
Buttons
4 marbles
Epoxy glue
Hot-glue gun and hot-glue sticks
Clear spray acrylic sealer
Child's spoon

now make it together

1 Base-coat the wood box with a color of your choice. Let it dry.

2 Spray the box with acrylic sealer. Let it dry.

3 Turn the base of the box upside down and epoxy the marbles onto the four corners of the box (these will act as legs for the box). Let it dry.

4 Determine the placement of the spoon on the box lid. If desired, epoxy buttons on the lid to support the spoon handle. Glue the child's spoon on the middle of the box lid. Let it dry.

Bright Idea
....
Make a pen holder for Dad's desk using a can instead of a glass vase.

**Talk With
Your Kids**
....
Discuss
safety
in the
workshop
before
letting your
kids use
any tools.

Spoon Hook

Mom will always know
where to find her keys with
this fun hook.

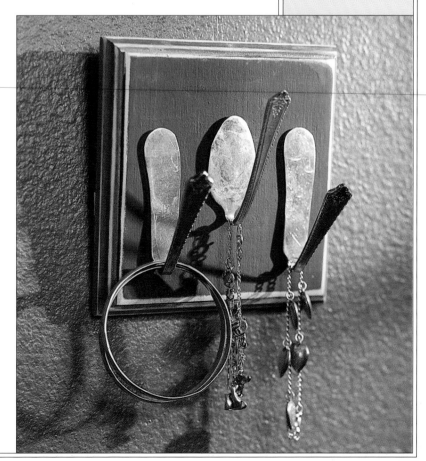

what you'll need

5½-inch wood plaque
Sawtooth picture hanger with nails
Acrylic paint; paintbrush
Clear spray acrylic sealer
Silver spoon and 2 butter knives
Epoxy glue
2 thick towels
Hammer

now make it together

1 Nail sawtooth picture hanger on back of
wood plaque.

2 Paint the wood plaque as desired. Let it
dry. Spray with acrylic sealer. Let dry.

3 Place the spoon and knives between two
thick towels. Hammer the silverware
until flat. Bend the pieces at the base of the
handle into a V shape. Glue the flattened
spoon and knife sections onto the plaque as
shown, *right*. Let it dry.

Ribbon Hangers

Celebrate the birthday of someone special by making a pair of these lovely ribbon-embroidered clothes hangers.

what you'll need

Fine straight pins
Embroidery floss
Silk embroidery ribbon in desired colors
Satin-covered padded clothes hangers
Needles—Milliner's #10, Chenille #18,
  and Embroidery #8
Seed beads, optional
Scissors; ¼-inch satin ribbon; thread; ruler

now make it together

1 Use straight pins to place green ribbon on hanger. Bend and twist the ribbon to form soft loops for leaves and curving branches. Thread the milliner's needle with thread and take a tiny tacking stitch to replace each straight pin. Tack only the base of each leaf loop. After you have completed the flowers, go back and tack down the leaves.

2 **To Make a Gathered Flower,** sew the ends of a 2- to 4-inch length of ribbon together with thread. Take tiny running stitches in one edge of the ribbon. Gently pull up the thread to form a circle. Do not cut the thread or remove the needle. Pin the flower onto the hanger and tack in place. You may wish to sew on a bead to cover the center tacking stitches.

3 **To Make the Roses,** thread a 12-inch length of embroidery floss in the embroidery needle. Determine placement and size of roses. From the center to the outside edge of the rose, take five evenly spaced stitches to create five spokes of a spider's web. Tie off embroidery thread behind a leaf loop or in the back of the hanger. Use a 15-inch length of ribbon in a chenille needle and come up as close to the center of the flower as possible without going through any embroidery threads. Weave the ribbon over and under the spokes until you no longer see them. To end off, take the needle through the hanger fabric under the last petal. Tie off under a leaf loop or in the back of the hanger.

4 **For French Knot Flowers,** bring the silk ribbon up through the fabric, wrapping the ribbon around the needle once and bringing the point of the needle back to the fabric next to where it was brought up. Before taking the needle back down, tighten the wrap gently around the needle. Different size knots are created by adjusting how tight or loose you make the wrap.

5 Tack down the leaves to hide ribbon ends. Tie a satin bow at the bottom of the hook.

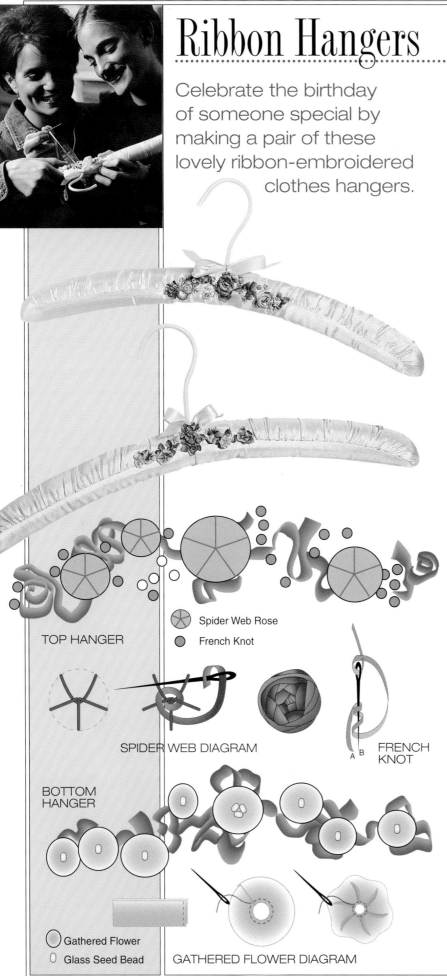

TOP HANGER

⚝ Spider Web Rose

⬤ French Knot

SPIDER WEB DIAGRAM

FRENCH KNOT

BOTTOM HANGER

◯ Gathered Flower

0 Glass Seed Bead

GATHERED FLOWER DIAGRAM

Happy Birthday Candleholders

Make it a birthday to remember with these delicate blooms that hold the candles.

what you'll need

Polymer clay, such as Sculpey III, in two desired colors and green
Tiny cookie or canapé cutters, such as Friendly Cutters, in flower and leaf shapes
Needle; birthday cake candle
White or clear plastic lid from a coffee can
Thick white crafts glue
Scissors
Spray varnish
Rolling pin, optional

now make it together

1 Knead the clay until soft. Flatten a piece of clay with fingers or a rolling pin.

2 Cut two flowers, one from each color of clay; make one flower slightly smaller than the other. With thumb, flatten petals of the larger flower. Use the edge of a needle to mark veins in each petal. Pull up the edges of the petals on the smaller flower.

3 Place small flower on top of large flower. Push a birthday candle into the center of the top flower, pushing through to the larger flower but not all the way out the bottom of the larger flower. Remove candle.

4 Cut two leaves from green clay, using needle to draw veins along leaf. Position leaves under flower, gently rubbing edges into the bottom of the flower.

5 Bake in the oven according to the directions on the clay package. Cool.

6 Spray the flower candleholders with varnish. Let them dry.

7 Cut a circle from the plastic lid just large enough for the flower to sit on. Glue it to the bottom of the flower and leaf. Make as many candleholders as needed.

Talk With Your Kids

····

Talk about memorable birthdays— gifts you received and the people who shared your day.

Sturdy-as-a-Rock Paperweight

Say "Happy Father's Day" by making your Dad his favorite animal to use as a weight for all his important papers.

what you'll need
Rocks
Strong adhesive, such as E6000
Acrylic paint in desired colors
Paintbrush
Glitter glue
Chenille stems
Scissors
Felt

now make it together

1 Arrange small rocks to look like a turtle, ladybug, or other character. Glue the rocks together. Let the rocks dry.

2 FOR THE LADYBUG, paint the body red, the head black, and the eyes white. Let the paint dry. Paint a black line down the center of the body. Paint black dots on the eyes and on the body. Paint a white smile.

Use glitter glue to make circles around the black dots on the body. Let dry.

3 FOR THE TURTLE, paint the body green, the head and feet brown, the nose red, and the eyes white. Let the paint dry. Paint brown dots randomly on the body and on the top portion of the eyes. Paint black dots below the eyelids. Paint a black smile and black details on the feet. Use glitter glue to draw between the circles on the body as shown, *left.* Let dry.

4 If desired, add antennae by twisting a chenille stem around the creature's neck and twisting the ends.

5 Cut a piece of felt to fit the bottom of the paperweight. Glue in place. Let dry.

Autographed Baseball

Remind Dad how much he means to you with this personalized baseball that sends dear sentiments.

what you'll need

Baseball
Pencil
Black and red paint markers
Candleholder
Colored wire or ribbon
Scissors

now make it together

1 Write a message on the baseball with pencil first so you can erase any mistakes. Write over the pencil with paint markers. Let it dry. Add hearts or other designs around the writing. Let it dry.

2 Place the baseball on a candleholder. Tie a wire or ribbon bow around the stem of the holder. Trim the ribbon ends if desired.

Big Hug Greeting Card

When two arms just aren't enough for hugging, add two more with this hug-in-a-card for Dad.

what you'll need
4 sheets of printer paper
Construction paper
Scissors
Markers, colored pencils, crayons, stickers
Transparent tape
Thick white crafts glue

now make it together

1 Tape four sheets of printer paper together, end to end. Lay the paper on the floor or a table, and have someone help you trace around one hand and arm to cover half the paper. On the opposite end of the paper, trace around the other hand and arm. Connect the two tracings in the center with tape. Cut out the arms.

2 Use markers, colored pencils, crayons, and/or stickers to decorate the card. Write a message across the arms.

3 Accordion-fold the arms until one hand stacks on the other.

4 Fold a 14×7-inch piece of construction paper in half. Write a message on the outside of the card.

5 Attach the hug inside the card by gluing the bottom hand on the right side of the greeting card.

Stick People Glassware

Create unique glassware for Dad using your own playful artwork designs.

what you'll need
Scissors
Stick people art
Masking tape
Plain glass cake stand
Plain, clear drinking glasses
Various colors gloss glass paint, such as Deco Art
Liner paintbrush

now make it together

1 Have your kids draw stick figures on paper. Place the drawing inside the glass or cake dome and tape it down.

2 Paint the stick figures by tracing the image taped to the glass. Follow the instructions on the paint bottle. Let the paint dry. Paint the stem of the cake plate if desired. Remove patterns. Bake the painted glassware in the oven if directed by the paint manufacturer. Let the glassware cool.

Talk With Your Kids
· · · ·
Spend time looking at and discussing your kids' artwork from various periods of their lives. Frame two or three favorites for the family to admire.

**Bright
Idea**
• • • •
Let each
family
member
make a
garden
plaque and
arrange in
the garden
as
stepping-
stones.

Playful Garden Plaques

Personalize a garden stone for Dad that will last through all the seasons.

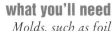

what you'll need

*Molds, such as foil pie tins
Newspapers
Quick-drying concrete
Plastic work container
Water*

*Rocks, marbles, small toys, or other items
Nonstick cooking spray; acrylic paints; paintbrush*

now make it together

1 In a well-ventilated work area, place newspapers over work surface.

2 Pour quick-drying concrete into a plastic container. For each tin, you'll need about 8 cups of dry concrete mix. Mix it with water according to the directions. To slow the drying time, add another cup of water to the mixture. Just before you pour, spray the form with nonstick cooking spray. When the mixture is the consistency of cake batter, pour it carefully into the form.

3 Smooth out the concrete and add embellishments, such as rocks, marbles, or small toys. Write your name with a small stick and make a handprint or footprint if desired. Work quickly. Wash hands or feet when done. Let the plaque dry.

4 Remove the plaque from the form. Paint it as desired. Let the paint dry.

Around-the-World Stamp Box

Recycle canceled stamps to make a one-of-a-kind box for good ol' Dad.

what you'll need

Postage stamps, postmarked or new
Small scissors
Glossy decoupage medium
Paintbrush
Star-shape cardboard box with lid

now make it together

1 If using recycled postage stamps, carefully remove them from postcards and envelopes. It is OK if some of the paper sticks to the back of the stamp. Be sure the paper is removed from the edges so it doesn't show from the front. Carefully trim the paper away if needed.

2 Working on small sections at a time, brush decoupage medium on the cardboard box. Paint decoupage medium on the back of the stamps and place randomly on the box and lid. Layer the stamps, turning them in all directions and overlapping the edges. Cover the entire outside surface. Let the decoupage medium dry.

3 Paint a coat of decoupage medium over all of the areas covered with stamps. Let the box dry.

summer

School's out, the sun is shining, and everyone's more eager than ever to spend quality time together. Come along and celebrate the kick-back days of summer by creating fun-in-the-sun projects to use and enjoy. Together we'll make fantastic animals, clever noisemakers, great stuff for summertime trips—even T-shirts and camp-out projects to help make the most of your treasured vacation days.

crafting in summer

With oodles of free time on your hands, you can make this a summer to remember forever. Whether you plan to take a trip to the beach or spend your warm-weather days in the backyard, here are some wonderful ideas to spark your creativity for summer crafting. So gather the family together and get ready to make memories.

◆ Purchase several inexpensive terra-cotta flowerpots to decorate for summer plants and flowers. Use paints to personalize the pots or glue on trims, such as ribbons, buttons, charms, or wood cutouts.

◆ Plan a Saturday just for checking out garage sales. Keep an eye out for chairs, benches, small tables, and other items to repaint for decorating your home indoors and out.

◆ When you take your next summer drive, be sure to tote along a car-friendly craft. Sewing, beading, and paper crafts help pass the time when traveling. Store your supplies for the car in a small plastic box with a lid.

◆ Make plans to visit a beach and take along a pail for collecting shells, rocks, driftwood, and other treasures. Check local restrictions before taking these items home.

◆ Spruce up your landscaping by making rock creatures, small signs, and stepping-stones. Take a trip to your local garden center to gather ideas.

◆ Plan a picnic in the park and be sure to pack watercolor paints, colored pencils, or crayons for the trip. Have each family member draw something beautiful he or she sees.

◆ Take time to organize your crafts supplies. Purchase a few plastic boxes to sort your items, then make labels for each box so you can gather items for a project without sifting through all your supplies.

◆ Purchase picture frames to decorate; then gather favorite photographs from your summer vacation and frame them to enjoy all year long.

◆ Let each family member buy a new pair of sunglasses. Make cases for each pair from bright felt rectangles stitched together on three sides with embroidery floss. For extra sparkle, the kids can decorate their shades with gems glued onto the frames with jewel glue.

◆ As you head out to your favorite river, lake, or ocean, be sure to talk about water safety. To guard against sunburn, decorate an umbrella to stick in the sand next to your beach blanket.

◆ Make supper time special by decorating silverware handles with oven-bake clay, such as Sculpey. Choose bright summer colors to make flowers, bugs, or geometric designs from the clay.

◆ Pick a fresh bouquet to display in an unexpected flea market find, such as a milk bottle or rusted pail.

◆ To make garden markers, decoupage seed packet fronts to a small rectangle of wood; attach to a dowel.

◆ To make a fun swim tote, purchase a canvas bag at your local crafts shop. Draw a simple design on one side, such as flowers, fish, or circles. Use beads and embroidery floss to embellish the designs.

◆ Welcome birds to your yard with a one-of-a-kind house just for them. Purchase a plain wood birdhouse and paint it with acrylic paints.

◆ Glued with construction adhesive, various sizes of terra-cotta flowerpots stack nicely to form bases for birdbaths, flowerpot and luminaria stands, and garden gazing balls.

◆ Purchase white T-shirts and have a tie-dying party outdoors. After the shirts dry, each guest can take his or her creation home to wear all summer long.

Summer Sketch Chair

Whether parked on the patio or next to your favorite fishing hole, these playful chairs show off your kids' works of art!

what you'll need

Spray paint in desired color for chair
New or recycled folding chair
Kids' fish drawing
Pencil
Tracing paper
Transfer paper
Acrylic enamel paints in desired colors
Paintbrush

now make it together

1 In a well-ventilated work area, spray-paint the chair a favorite color. Let the paint dry.

2 Trace your fish drawing onto tracing paper. Keep in mind that the drawing, or a portion of it, must fit on the chair back. Use transfer paper to transfer the design to the chair back.

3 Paint the design using the desired colors. Let the paint dry.

4 Outline desired areas of the design using black. Let the paint dry.

Sunshine Sandals

Have fun in the sun with these brightly painted summer flip-flops!

what you'll need

Vinyl sandals
Acrylic enamel paints in purple, pink, white, orange, and lime green
Dimensional fabric paint in lime green, optional
Paintbrush
Comb
Rag

now make it together

1 Your sandals can be smooth or can have grooves and stripes in them like these. Follow the texture in the sandals to make your design, if desired. Wash and dry the sandals.

2 Paint the entire top of each sandal purple. Let the paint dry.

3 Paint stripes of pink and orange as desired. Let the paint dry.

4 Paint checks or dots over the solid colors. To make dots, dip the handle of a paintbrush in paint and dot onto the surface.

5 To make stripes with tiny vertical lines, first paint the base pink color. Let it dry (this is important so the paint doesn't scratch off). Paint green over the pink. Comb over the wet green paint to take away the green and let the pink lines show through. Wipe the paint off the comb between each pass of the comb. You can also use dimensional fabric paint for the top layer when combing. Fabric paint is thicker and works well for making a distinctive texture.

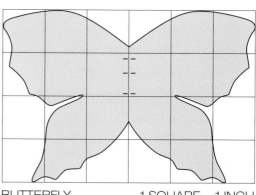

Bright Idea
....
Experiment with making other insects for the mobile, such as fireflies, ladybugs, and bees.

Butterfly Mobile

Bring summer indoors by decorating your room with a mobile of floating butterflies.

what you'll need

2-foot-long piece of ¼-inch dowel
3 straws; colored thread; printer paper
6 cotton swabs
Watercolor paints; paintbrush
Crayons
Six 3-inch-long pieces of coated telephone wire or twist ties; scissors; ruler

now make it together

1 Enlarge and trace the butterfly pattern, *right*, onto printer paper six times, varying the wing shapes as desired.

2 Cut out the shapes and make small slits where indicated on the pattern. Color both sides, pressing hard with crayon so the color won't wash away. Brush on watercolor paint, using just a small amount of water on the brush. Let dry and repeat on other side.

3 Use watercolors to paint cotton swab and dowel, if desired. Let them dry.

4 Thread cotton swabs through slits in wings. For antennae, bend wire in half and twist around swab. Curl ends with your fingers.

5 Cut six 8-inch-long pieces of thread. Tie one thread end to the wire antennae. Tie the other end to last slit in the wing. Make 1-inch slits on each end of the straws. Slide the butterfly strings onto the straws. Tie the straws to the dowel.

BUTTERFLY PATTERN   1 SQUARE = 1 INCH

Friendly Fireflies

These luminous glowworms will love lighting up the evening sky!

what you'll need

9×12-inch sheet of construction paper
16-oz. green plastic soda bottle
Tape; 2 chenille stems; pencil; tracing paper
Scissors; thick white crafts glue
Pom-poms
Fluorescent light stick (available wherever camping supplies are sold)
Colorful construction paper

now make it together

1 Fold the construction paper in half lengthwise and tear it along the fold. Wrap one half around the bottle top for the bug's thorax and tape it in place.

2 Wrap a chenille stem around the bottle neck and twist it to make antennae.

Cut the other chenille stem into thirds and glue the pieces onto the sides of the bottle for the legs.

3 Trace the circle and wing patterns, *below,* onto tracing paper. Cut out the patterns. Trace around the patterns on construction paper, cutting one circle face and two wings. Cut out the shapes. Glue the wings to the thorax. Glue the circle on the bottle cap for a face. Add pom-poms for the eyes. Let the glue dry.

4 Activate the light stick and place it inside the bottle.

Talk With Your Kids
. . . .
Research fireflies to learn how they glow and what they look like up close.

CIRCLE
FACE
PATTERN

FIREFLY
WING
PATTERN

Pet Necklace

Keep a close reminder of your furry family member by making a necklace with the features of your adorable pet.

what you'll need

FOR THE CAT
DMC pearl cotton #3 in color #947
Acrylic paint in rust, orange, white, red, and pink; paintbrush
Permanent, black fine-point marker
Wood beads—one 20mm head, one 26mm body, four 10mm paws, twelve 8mm arms and legs; crewel needle
9mm gold split ring; thick white crafts glue
Wood buttons—two 4-hole, two 2-hole
Orange crafting foam; scissors; yardstick
Cording; alphabet beads

FOR THE DOG
DMC pearl cotton #3 in color #434
Acrylic paint in terra-cotta, red, white, pink, and blue; paintbrush
Permanent, black fine-point marker
Wood beads—one 20mm head, six 10mm paws and legs, ten 8mm arms and legs, and one 26mm body
Crewel needle; thick white crafts glue
9mm gold split ring
Wood buttons—two 4-hole, two 2-hole
Dark brown crafting foam; scissors, yardstick
Cording; alphabet beads

now make it together

1 **FOR THE CAT,** paint six 8mm beads rust, six 8mm beads orange, four 10mm beads white, a 20mm and a 26mm bead orange, a 4-hole button rust, a 4-hole button orange, and two 2-hole buttons white. Let dry.

2 **FOR THE DOG,** paint ten 8mm beads terra-cotta, four 10mm beads white, two 10mm beads terra-cotta, a 20mm and a 26mm bead terra-cotta, a 4-hole button blue, a 4-hole button terra-cotta, and two 2-hole buttons white. Let dry.

3 Using guides, *below,* paint features. Use patterns to cut, paint, and glue on foam ears or mane pieces. To assemble, thread a 60-inch strand of pearl cotton on a crewel needle. Run through split ring; then run both ends through head bead. (Rethreading needle is necessary for working body.) Thread one strand on needle and run through one hole of 4-hole button. Thread on second strand and run through hole opposite on button. On same thread, string three 8mm beads and a 10mm bead. Run needle back through three 8mm beads. Run needle back into buttonhole next to beaded strand. Pull out through top of head, reinsert over split ring, and bring back down through head and button. Repeat for second arm. Pick up both strands and run through body bead. Pick up one strand, run through button, and thread on leg beads. *For dog,* string on a 10mm bead, two 8mm beads, and one 10mm bead. *For cat,* string on three 8mm beads and a 10mm bead. *For both characters,* draw down through 2-hole button and draw back through button, leg beads, and base button. Tie off when legs are complete. String on cording with alphabet beads.

DOG PAINTING GUIDE

CAT PAINTING GUIDE

DOG EAR

CAT BELLY

CAT MANE

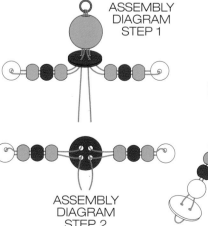

ASSEMBLY DIAGRAM STEP 1

ASSEMBLY DIAGRAM STEP 2

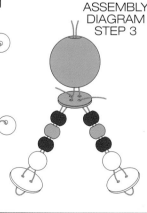

ASSEMBLY DIAGRAM STEP 3

Pet Jar Topper

Keep treats for kitty or puppy handy in a jar topped with a clay rendition of your cuddly companion.

what you'll need

Jar with wood lid; drill and drill bit
Fine sandpaper; 1½-inch wood screw
Acrylic paint in light green, dark green,
  yellow, white, light brown, dark brown,
  cream, black, pink, red, gold, and rust
Air-dry clay, such as Crayola Model Magic clay

now make it together

1 Remove the wood lid from the jar. Mark the center of the lid. Drill a small hole where marked.

2 If the lid has a sealer or paint on it, lightly sand it so the paint will adhere. Paint the lid light green. Let dry. Using the photo, *above*, paint dots and a flower design on the lid. To paint dots, dip the handle of a paintbrush into paint and dot onto the surface. To make flower petals, lay a small round paintbrush on its side. Let the paint dry.

3 Using clay, create the animal shapes. Use golf-ball-size balls for the bodies. Roll small snake shapes for the arms, legs, and tails. Flatten small balls for the paws and facial features. Shape small triangles for the cat's ears. Press shapes together. Poke the handle of a small paintbrush 1 inch into the bottom of the animal. Remove paintbrush. Let the clay dry.

4 Paint the clay animals as desired using the photos for inspiration. Let dry.

5 From the bottom, screw a wood screw through the hole in the lid. Screw the clay animal onto the lid.

Buster Bowl

Personalize a bowl for your pup by painting on bright designs and his name.

what you'll need
Dog food bowl
Acrylic enamel paints in desired colors
Paintbrush

now make it together

1 Wash the dog food bowl. Let it dry. Avoid touching the areas to be painted.

2 Paint the dog's name on the bowl as desired. You can tilt some of the letters as shown, *left;* then add painted lines above or below the letters. Paint stripes around the bottom edge of the bowl.

3 Paint desired motifs around the bowl. Make squiggles, zigzags, or any other desired shapes. Let the paint dry.

Doggone Dining Delight

With a mat and a dish to call his own, your canine friend will be dining in style!

Poochy Place Mat

what you'll need
Crafting foam
Scissors; thick white crafts glue

now make it together

1 Cut out letters and the shapes of bones, paws, and hearts from foam.

2 Glue the shapes around the sides and top of a full sheet of foam using the photo, *right,* for ideas.

Gus Bowl

what you'll need
Pencil; dog food bowl; biscuit, fabric paint pens

now make it together

1 Write your pet's name on his food bowl with a pencil. Trace one of his biscuits all around the rest of the bowl.

2 Paint the biscuits and name with fabric paint pens. Let the paint dry. Paint "YUM" on each biscuit. Let it dry.

Bright Idea
····
Use this place mat idea to make mats for your own table. Instead of bones and dog prints, choose motifs such as the sun, flowers, beach balls, and stars.

Kitty Climber

Covered in soft carpeting, this kitty post is ready for play!

what you'll need

½-inch-thick wood large enough to cut a 16-inch square, a 12-inch square, and an 8-inch-wide circle
8-inch-wide cardboard tubular cement form
Saw; yardstick
Carpet scrap large enough to cover squares
Staple gun and staples
100 yards of sisal rope
Scissors; wood glue
Tape
Strong adhesive, such as Liquid Nails

now make it together

1 Cut two wood squares, 16 and 12 inches square. Trace the inside of the tube onto wood and cut out.

2 Cut the tube to desired height (ours is 16 inches). You can make these tall, as long as they have a larger base to keep them from tipping over. Cut a square opening in the tube large enough for a cat.

3 Tape one end of sisal rope onto the tube flush with the edge of tube. Spread a generous amount of wood glue onto tube and begin winding sisal tightly around tube. Continue winding even around opening, until you cover the entire tube. Tape the end in place. Let the sisal firmly dry.

4 Lay carpet down, back side up. Lay boards down onto carpet. Cut out two squares of carpet, leaving a 3-inch trim around each side.

5 With large carpet piece back side up, lay the tube in the center. Trace around tube and cut out the hole.

6 Glue with adhesive or nail the circle board onto the center of the 16-inch board.

7 The sisal should be dry now. Finish the opening. Cut each piece of sisal at the edge of the opening. Use tape to hold the edges intact. Tape firmly from the outside into the inside of the tube.

8 Position the tube onto the wooden circle so that it sits nicely in place. Pull the carpet with hole cut out over the tube and lay it smoothly down in place. Staple at least 4 staples around the edge of the circle opening. Now you can temporarily remove the tube.

9 Turn the board over. Begin at one end, pulling the carpet around the edge, stapling as you go. Staple one side, then the opposite side. Do this until complete on both pieces of wood.

10 Use strong adhesive to glue around the inside of the tube at the base to hold it in place. You may also glue any carpet scrap pieces to the inside of the tube for your cat to have better traction on the inside.

11 Glue around the top rim of tube, add carpeted top with wood side down, and reinforce with several staples.

Note: Hang feathers or toys from your cat post if desired.

Talk With Your Kids
····
Talk about the different varieties of cats, including those you see at the zoo.

Bright Idea
••••
Make message necklaces for special friends and relatives at times such as Valentine's Day, Mother's Day, and Friendship Day.

Colorful Collar of Love

A handmade gift will show your pet just how special he is.

what you'll need

⅛-inch-wide suede shoelace; scissors
Wood beads, round and square
6×9mm plastic pony beads
Small bell
Paintbrush; acrylic paints in light colors
Black marker; ruler
Lanyard hook and a 16mm (⅝-inch) ring

now make it together

1 Cut the shoelace to fit comfortably around your pet's neck plus about 3 inches. Plan the words you want on the collar—your pet's name or something like "My pal" or "Pet me."

2 Line up the wood beads and the bell along the shoelace with a pony bead between the big pieces, but don't string them on the lace yet. Paint the wood beads. Let them dry. Write the same letter on the four solid sides of each cube so they'll appear right side up on the collar.

3 String all the beads on the shoelace. Wrap one end of the shoelace around the lanyard hook and push it into the nearest bead. Attach the ring in the same way at the other end.

Note: Keep a close eye on your pets when they're wearing special collars. Don't let them chew on the parts.

Kitty Hanky Pillow

This soft pillow, made from vintage hankies, will surely make your kitty purr.

what you'll need

8 clean, ironed vintage handkerchiefs
Thread
Needle
Square pillow form
  slightly smaller
  than pillow top
1/8-inch satin ribbon
Scissors
Basket the approximate size
  of the pillow form

now make it together

1 Choose four hankies for the pillow top and four for the bottom. On a flat work surface, arrange the hankies for each layer into a square.

2 For each layer, stitch the corners of the hankies together. With the wrong sides of the hankies facing, place a pillow form between the hankies.

3 Stitch the hankies together at the corners and sides using running stitches.

4 Tie ribbon bows around the corners of the pillow. Trim the ribbon ends if needed. Place the pillow in a basket that is approximately the size of the pillow.

Talk With Your Kids
....
Talk about pets—how they differ and how they're the same.

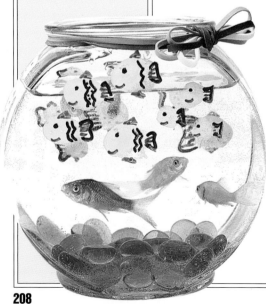

Bright Idea

····

For a fun party centerpiece, paint a large fishbowl and fill with miniature candy bars.

Swishy Fishy Bowls

Give your smallest pet company by painting a school of little swimmers on a glass fishbowl.

what you'll need

Fishbowl
Glass paints in desired colors; paintbrush
Paper plate
Colored rubber bands

now make it together

1 Wash the fishbowl. Let it dry. Avoid touching the areas to be painted.

2 Place a small amount of paint on the plate to be used for the fish bodies. Dip your finger into paint and press horizontally on the fishbowl. Continue making fingerprint fish until you have approximately a dozen fish bodies painted on the bowl. Let the paint dry.

3 Use contrasting colors of paints to add details to the fish as shown, *left*. Let the paint dry.

4 Group a few rubber bands, securing in the middle to create a bow. Tuck three or four rubber bands through center of bow. Pull loop ends through opposite loops to secure. Attach to the rim.

Pet Frame

Show off photos of your finicky feline or playful pooch in a frame that is created just for your pet.

Talk With Your Kids
····
Have fun thinking up silly pet names for dogs, cats, birds, and fish.

what you'll need

Computer to print out words
Scissors
Magazines
Newspapers
Glue stick
Typing paper
Decoupage medium
Paintbrush
Frame
Picture mat, if desired

now make it together

1 If you have a computer available, print out desired words, such as *cat*, *dog*, or *friends*, in different fonts, sizes, and colors. If you don't have a computer, clip out these words from magazines and newspapers. If you want more than one copy, glue the word(s) on a piece of typing paper and have copies made at a copy center.

2 To include photos or pictures, clip them out of magazines or have color copies made of your own photos.

3 Cover your work surface with newspapers. To decoupage the words or pictures on a frame, trim the pieces as you like and decide where you want to put them. Brush decoupage medium over the frame. To add cutouts, brush the back side with decoupage medium and smooth onto the frame or mat. Wrap the cutouts around the center opening and edges. Overlap pieces as you wish. Continue adding cutouts until the entire frame or mat is covered. Let the glue dry.

4 Before applying decoupage medium over the top of the cutouts, test it on an extra cutout to be sure it doesn't make the colors bleed. If it doesn't bleed, paint decoupage medium over all of the cutouts. Let it dry.

Souvenir-of-Summer Shirt

Turn a favorite vacation memory into a unique shirt to wear all summer long.

Bright Idea
••••
Make everyone in the family a matching T-shirt for your next family reunion.

what you'll need

T-shirt; new sponge
Acrylic or dimensional paints
Assortment of shells or other souvenir objects
Paintbrush

now make it together

1 Lay the T-shirt on a table. Place the sponge inside the T-shirt right under the spot you want to paint.

2 Squeeze a little paint on the shell (or other object) you want to use as a block print and use a brush to spread the paint around. Press the shell onto the shirt over the sponge. The sponge will help balance the shell on the shirt. Repeat the process with different colors, moving the sponge each time.

3 Paint a favorite saying on the shirt if desired. Let the paint dry.

Seashore Jewelry

Whether found at the ocean's edge or purchased from a store, these interesting shells make one-of-a-kind jewelry.

Seashore Necklace

what you'll need

*Small starfish; white acrylic paint; paintbrush
Iridescent white glitter; thick white crafts glue
Eye pin; beading string or dental floss; ruler
Scissors; beading needle
Pastel pearl beads; end clasps for necklaces*

now make it together

1 Paint the starfish white. Let dry. Paint a second coat. Sprinkle white glitter onto the wet paint. Shake off the excess. Let dry.

2 Use crafts glue to attach a small eye pin to the back of the starfish. When the glue dries, add a little more glue and let it dry.

3 Cut an 18-inch-long piece of beading string or dental floss. Tie one of the end clasps to the end of the string. Thread the other string end through the needle.

4 Lay beads out in the order you want them, making a line about 14 inches long. Find the middle of the line of beads and place the starfish there.

5 Begin to string on the beads in the order you have decided. When you get to the middle, string on the decorated starfish. Continue stringing beads. Tie end to clasp.

Seashore Pin

what you'll need

*Acrylic paint in white and white pearl
Paintbrush; 1¼-inch square of cardboard
Clamshell; thick white crafts glue
Small pastel-painted shells
Pin back; hot-glue gun; hot-glue sticks*

now make it together

1 Paint one side of the cardboard white. Let dry. Paint the other side white and let dry.

2 Paint the clamshell with a coat of white pearl paint. Let it dry. Paint another coat if needed. Let it dry.

3 Coat one side of the square with a generous amount of crafts glue. Place the painted clamshell in the center of the glued square. Fill in the rest of the square with tiny shells. Let it dry overnight.

4 Hot-glue the pin back to the top back side of the square. Let it dry.

Seashore Barrette

what you'll need

*Acrylic paint in white pearl and pink pearl
Paintbrush; two 1-inch shells
24 tiny shells with drilled holes
Pastel seed beads; beading thread
Hot-glue gun; hot-glue sticks; barrette back*

now make it together

1 Paint two 1-inch-size shells with white pearl paint and 24 tiny shells with pink pearl paint. Let the paint dry.

2 String seed beads onto thread, ending with a small pink shell. Make approximately a dozen strings of various lengths.

3 With the shell ends down, hot-glue the tops of the strings to the center of the barrette. Glue the larger white shells on the string ends. Glue the remaining shells to the ends of the barrette, along with beads if desired. Let the glue dry.

Talk With Your Kids

••••

Surf the Internet to find pictures of various seashells. Find out where different types are found and what items are made from them.

**Bright
Idea**
• • • •
To make
drums with
a different
sound, use
jingle bells
where the
beads are
placed.

Bead Drum

Get your family band jamming with bead drums made from items found around the house.

what you'll need

2 sturdy paper plates; markers
Paper punch
9 wood beads
Twine (nine 10-inch lengths)
Thick white crafts glue
Dowel; ruler

now make it together

1 With markers, make colorful patterns on the outside of each paper plate.

2 Holding the plates together with the tops facing, punch nine holes equally spaced around the edges. Tie a length of twine through each hole, knotting it at the hole and leaving the ends about 4 inches long. Thread a bead onto one of the ends and tie the two ends together, leaving ends about ½-inch long.

3 Glue a dowel between the plates. Let the glue dry.

Rubber Band Band

Whether used to add decorative stripes to a shaker or for making the pleasant twangs of a string instrument, rubber bands are a hit in this musical duo.

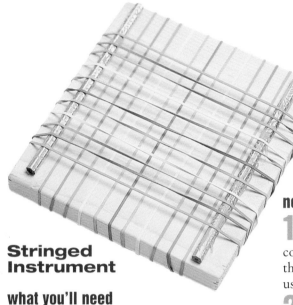

Stringed Instrument

what you'll need

2 decorative pencils
Hacksaw
7×7-inch piece of wood
Hot-glue gun and hot-glue sticks
Colored rubber bands

now make it together

1 Saw the eraser ends off two pencils. Hot-glue the pencils to one side of the wood piece as shown in the photo, *above.* Let the glue dry.

2 Place rubber bands over the wood, parallel to the pencils. Place rubber bands over the wood piece in the opposite direction, so they rest on the pencils. To make sounds, pluck or strum the top layer of rubber bands.

Shaker

what you'll need

1 cup uncooked popcorn, rice, or dried beans
Tall stacked-chip container with lid
Packing tape; ice pick; pencil
Jute rope; scissors
Hot-glue gun and hot-glue sticks
Colored rubber bands
Thin, colored metallic wire
Wire cutters; ruler

now make it together

1 Place popcorn, rice, or dried beans in the container. Tape the lid to the container. Using an ice pick, poke a hole in the center of the lid. Make the hole larger using a pencil.

2 Place the end of the jute into the hole in the lid. Begin wrapping the jute around and around, gluing as you work. Continue wrapping the lid, sides, and bottom of the container until covered. Clip the jute and glue the end to secure.

3 To make rubber band bows, group a dozen rubber bands. Wrap the center with a 6-inch length of wire to secure. Make three bows. Glue the bows to one side of the shaker.

In-the-Swim Beach Pail

This bright beach pail carries your gear to the shore and then holds found treasures to carry back home.

what you'll need

Pail
Acrylic paints in desired colors; paintbrush
Pencil; tracing paper; scissors; jumbo rickrack

now make it together

1 Paint the background areas of the pail, painting a yellow stripe on the top and bottom with white in between. Let dry.

2 Trace the patterns, *below.* Cut out. Trace around the shapes on the pail using the photo, *left,* as a guide. For the zigzag, trace the edges of a piece of jumbo rickrack. Paint in the details. Let dry.

BEACH PAIL FISH AND
BUBBLE PATTERNS

Map-It-Out Car Caddy

Just the right size for travel games, maps, and car snacks, these take-along totes are a world of fun to make.

Talk With Your Kids
. . . .
Talk about a map of your city or state—how to read it and what the symbols mean. Then see who can refold it!

what you'll need

Maps or old atlas
Scissors
Glossy decoupage medium
Paintbrush
Carrying case, small toolbox, or other
  small case
Neck chain
Pony beads in desired colors
Small flashlight

now make it together

1 Use scissors to cut sections from maps or pages from an atlas. To apply each piece to the case, paint the back side with decoupage medium. Place on the case, trimming as necessary to fit around the hardware. Align the straight edges with the edges of the case that meet. Cover the entire case with map sections. Let the decoupage medium dry.

2 Paint a top coat of decoupage medium over all mapped areas. Let it dry. Apply another coat if desired and let dry.

3 String pony beads on the neck chain. Thread through a hole in the flashlight handle and attach it to the case handle.

Nature Bracelets

Pack a roll of wide masking tape with your family's camping supplies to make nature bracelets wherever you go.

what you'll need

Nature finds, such as bird feathers, dandelions, clover, ferns, leaves, baby pinecones, bits of moss, pebbles, curly twigs, tiny flowers, and flower petals
Masking tape

now make it together

1 Place a ring of masking tape, sticky side out, around your wrist. For comfort and to prevent the tape from tearing, leave some room for your wrist to bend.

2 Collect nature finds from the ground. As you collect these things, gently press them on the sticky tape until you have filled the entire bracelet.

Bark Frames

Collect tree bark—from the ground only, please—on your next camping trip and make a photo frame by gluing the bark to some type of stiff, flat backing.

what you'll need

Sturdy cardboard or heavy mat-board frame
Crafts knife; ruler
Pencil; paper
Tree bark
Thick white crafts glue
Waxed paper; photo

now make it together

1 To make the backing, cut a 5×7-inch frame (with a 3×5-inch window) from sturdy cardboard or use a precut, heavy mat-board frame. Trace the frame onto a plain piece of paper.

2 Arrange the bark on the paper tracing, fitting pieces together and overlapping the bark until the frame is covered. Break the bark into smaller pieces, if necessary, to fill in the spaces.

3 Spread glue on the frame and move the bark from the tracing to the frame. Press to secure. Sandwich the frame between two pieces of waxed paper to prevent sticking and place under a stack of books to dry and flatten. Place photo in frame.

Camp Poncho

Keep warm on cool evenings with a blanket that doubles as a poncho.

what you'll need
Polar fleece blanket (about 46×68 inches)
Embroidery floss; darning needle
Assorted colored felt for patches
Dimensional paint; scissors, ruler

now make it together

1 For the poncho, make the opening for the head by folding the blanket in half. Make a 10-inch-long cut lengthwise along the fold in the center of the blanket. Make a small 2-inch slit down from the center opening. You may want to finish the cut edge with blanket stitches.

2 For the patches, cut rectangles, ovals, or circles from felt—about 6×4 inches or 5×5 inches. Use dimensional paint to write the name of the park and the date, and draw a design, such as a canoe, fire, or pine tree. Let dry. Sew onto the blanket with floss.

Scrapbooks

Keep your best-loved photos, artwork, and clippings organized for everyone to see in these cleverly made books.

what you'll need

Cardboard, 11×17 inches
Construction paper, 11×17 inches
Assorted photos, drawings, school papers, etc.
Paper punch
Glue stick
Twine, ribbon, or chenille stems
Stick, 12-inch ruler, or paintbrush

now make it together

1 Set cardboard on table and stack the desired number of 11×17-inch pages of construction paper on top.

2 For cover, glue together a collage of photos, drawings, or other designs. Place cover on top of pages.

3 Punch two holes about 6 inches apart through all layers.

4 Pull cord up from under the cardboard, through the pages and cover. Loop the cord over the spine (the stick, ruler, or paintbrush), thread it back down through the same hole, and tie the ends together. Repeat for the second hole.

Photo Diorama

You'll love filing your photos of family and friends with these cheery, art-embellished file folders.

what you'll need

5¼-inch expandable file; construction paper
Assortment of photos from same season and
   location (enlargements work best)
Tape; glue stick

now make it together

1 Cut a window in the front of the expandable file.

2 Cut out photographed people and tape the largest one in front (for example, girl on left in the photo at *right*). Attach the smaller photos of people to the back side of window (three kids on right in photo).

Tape a scenic photo to the inside back of file (boy on beach in center of photo).

3 Cut out paper into shapes of sun, clouds, and a crab. A small construction paper shovel and pail are added to the center of the folder in front of the scenic photo. The top right corner of the front panel is cut out to reveal a cloud and blue sky. Glue pieces in place.

Star-Studded Photo Stands

Sneak photos into small spaces with these sparkling, easy-to-make stands.

what you'll need

Drill; ½- to 1-inch dowel
Heavy-gauge wire; wire cutters; pliers
Purchased wood shapes
Acrylic paint in desired colors; paintbrush
   Star stickers

now make it together

1 Drill a ⅛-inch hole approximately 1 inch from the end of a dowel. Insert the end of the wire into the hole in the dowel. Hold the dowel tight or place it in a vise. Twist the wire around the dowel two or three times. Remove the loops from the dowel. Cut the wire tail 3 to 6 inches from coils. Use pliers to bend the top of the spring straight and to make the loops tight together. Straighten the opposite end of the wire so it can be inserted into the hole in the wood shape.

2 Paint the wood shape a solid color. Let it dry. Apply star stickers to the top and sides if desired.
   Drill a tiny hole in the center of the wood shape. Insert the wire end into the hole.

**Talk With
Your Kids**
· · · ·
Teach your kids how to use a camera. Give them each a roll of film to capture photos of their favorite people and animals.

index

index continued on page 222

glossary

Acrylic Paint—water-based, quick-drying paint that cleans up with soap and water. Some are developed for outdoor use while others are for interior use only.

Base Coat—a first coat of paint that is used to prepare a surface for more paint or to provide a background color.

Bleed—in crafting terms, when colors run together, usually referring to paint.

Chenille Stem—a velvety covered wire (pipe cleaner) that can be purchased in a variety of sizes and colors, including metallic. Some chenille stems are striped.

Decoupage—the technique of cutting out designs (usually from paper) and mounting them on a surface using decoupage medium or a half-and-half mixture of glue and water.

Disposable—something meant to be used once and then thrown away.

Dowel—a solid cylinder of wood that comes in many sizes.

Enamel Paint—a glossy, colored, opaque paint used to decorate a variety of surfaces. Enamel paint can be water- or oil-based.

Fringe—a border or trim of cords or threads, hanging loose or tied in bunches.

Gems—in crafting terms, a plastic rhinestone or smooth colorful stone that is backed with metallic silver to make it sparkle.

Glossy—having a smooth, shiny appearance or finish.

Iridescent—showing changes in color when seen from different angles.

Knead—to mix by pressing and squeezing materials, such as clay, together.

Pony Beads—colorful plastic beads (round and shapes), ranging from about the size of a pea to the size of a nickel, with a large hole in the center.

Technique—the method used to do artwork, such as cross-stitching, painting, or decoupaging.

Texture—the appearance or feel of a surface.

Tracing—drawing around an object or copying the lines of drawn art.

Tracing Paper—a thin sheet of semi-transparent paper used to trace drawings or patterns.

Varnish—a final finish, satin, semi-gloss, or gloss, that protects the surface.

Waxed Paper—available in rolls, this paper has a moisture-proof coating and is often used to cover a work surface when crafting.

sources

Beads *are available at most art, crafts, stitchery, and discount stores.*
FOR MORE INFORMATION, contact Gay Bowles Sales/Mill Hill at P.O. Box 1060, Janesville, WI 53547 or at www.millhill.com or call 800-356-9438.
ALSO CONTACT Westrim Trimming, Corporation at 9667 Cantoga Avenue, Chatsworth, CA 91331 or at www.westrimcrafts.com or call 818-998-8550.
ANOTHER BEAD SOURCE is Bodacious Beads, 1942 River Road, Des Plaines, IL 84769-7959.

Buttons *are available at most fabric, crafts, stitchery, and discount stores.*
FOR MORE INFORMATION, contact JHB International at 1955 S. Quince Street, Denver, CO 80231 or call 303-751-8100.

Clay *is available at most art, crafts, and discount stores.*
FOR MORE INFORMATION ON SCULPEY III CLAY, contact Polyform Products Co. at 1901 Estes Avenue, Elk Grove Village, IL 60007 or at www.sculpey.com.
FOR INFORMATION ON CRAYOLA MODEL MAGIC, contact www.crayola.com or call 800-CRAYOLA.

Decorative-Edge Scissors *are available at most art and crafts stores.*
FOR MORE INFORMATION, contact Fiskars Consumer Products at 305 84th Avenue South, Wausau, WI 54401 or at www.fiskars.com or call 715-842-2091.

Decorative Papers *are available at most art stores.*
FOR MORE INFORMATION, contact www.shoptheartstore.com.

Decoupage Medium *is available at most art, crafts, and discount stores.*
FOR MORE INFORMATION, contact Plaid Enterprises at P.O. Box 2835, Norcross, GA 30091 or call 800-842-4197.

Embroidery Floss *is available at most stitchery, discount, and crafts stores.*
FOR MORE INFORMATION, contact Anchor Consumer Service Department, at P.O. Box 27067, Greenville, SC 29616 or DMC at Port Kearney Building 10, South Kearney, NJ 07032-0650.
ALSO CONTACT Herrschners at 800-441-0838.

Leather Lacing *is available at most art and crafts stores.*
FOR MORE INFORMATION, contact www.michaels.com.

Paints *are available at most art and crafts stores.*
FOR MORE INFORMATION, contact Plaid Enterprises at P.O. Box 2835, Norcross, GA 30091 or call 800-842-4197. ALSO CONTACT DecoArt Paint at P.O. Box 386, Stanford KY 40484 or call 800-367-3047.
FOR MORE INFORMATION ON GLASS PAINTS, contact Delta Technical Coatings, Inc. at 2550 Pellissier Place, Whittier, CA 90601-1505 or call 800-423-4135.
ALSO CONTACT Liquitex Glossies at Binney & Smith, Inc., Easton, PA 18044-0431.

Ribbons *are available at fabric and crafts stores.*
FOR MORE INFORMATION, contact C. M. Offray & Son, Inc. at Route 24, Box 601, Chester, NJ 07930-0601 or call 908-879-4700.

Thick White Crafts Glue *is available at most art, crafts, and discount stores.*
FOR MORE INFORMATION, contact Aleene's Tacky Glue at www.duncancrafts.com.

Wire *is available at most art and crafts stores.*
FOR MORE INFORMATION ON METALLIC WIRE, contact Artistic Wire, Ltd., at P.O. Box 1347, Elmhurst, IL 60126 or at www.artisticwire.com or call 630-530-7567.
FOR MORE INFORMATION ON PLASTIC-COATED COLORED WIRE, contact Twisteez at www.twisteez.com.

Designers
Susan M. Banker, Heidi Boyd, Donna Chesnut, Carol Field Dahlstrom, Phyllis Dunstan, Ardith Field, Alexa Lett, Renee E. McAtee, Bob Riley, Barbara Sestok, Margaret Sindelar, Alice Wetzel

Photographers
Andy Lyons Cameraworks, Peter Krumhardt, Scott Little, Tom McWilliams

Photostyling
Carol Dahlstrom
Donna Chesnut, assistant